SEEING THE
UNSEEN

SEEING THE
UNSEEN

Learning to See with the Eyes of our Hearts

Bob Stoddard

XULON PRESS

Xulon Press
2301 Lucien Way #415
Maitland, FL 32751
407.339.4217
www.xulonpress.com

Printed in the United States of America.

Paperback ISBN-13: 978-1-6322-1994-7
eBook ISBN-13: 978-1-6322-1995-4

For my beloved grandchildren,
Elijah and Sunshine Stoddard

Your wholehearted love
has brought joy and healing to my heart.

May you both be richly blessed
at an early age
with heart eyes that clearly see.

Table of Contents

Introduction

The Great Depression of the 1930s, with its associated twenty-five percent unemployment rate, led to a nation caught in a struggle to survive. There was, however, an occasional ray of sunlight that penetrated the heavy clouds of discouragement and hopelessness. Although those rays of sunlight were not in the form of economic relief, they helped lift the somber mood of the people and gave them a taste of optimism for a potentially brighter future. One of those beams of sunlight appeared in the form of the thoroughbred racehorse Seabiscuit.

Why a racehorse? Why were millions caught up in the media frenzy surrounding Seabiscuit's every move? Why did they identify so closely with this horse? Why, in the midst of their despair, did Seabiscuit bring the people hope?

As a racehorse with a poor initial performance, Seabiscuit's owners had given up on him. American workers could relate because they also felt they had been given up on. Yet, the horse proved the critics wrong. He went on to rise above mediocrity to become one of the greatest racehorses of all time. Seabiscuit's wins gave people hope for their own downtrodden lives.

Seabiscuit experienced many consecutive losses before winning a few races. Even with a few wins under his belt, he had an inconsistent track record. Racehorse experts felt he had no promising future. Everyone had turned their backs on Seabiscuit—everyone, that is, except trainer Tom Smith. Owner Charles Howard hired Smith to find a horse that would become a consistent winner. Despite a thorough search, Smith found no horses he felt were worth his time or Howard's money ... until he saw Seabiscuit. Seabiscuit? Anyone who knew anything about racing had already given up on Seabiscuit. Seabiscuit was a waste of time and money. What in the world did Smith see in Seabiscuit? In her New York Times Bestseller, *Seabiscuit: An American Legend*, Laura Hillenbrand tells us. "Countless horsemen had run their eyes over that plain bay body. None of them had seen what Smith saw."[1] Like all the other owners and trainers before him, "Smith saw the bucked knees, the insistent pressure of the ribs under skin, the weariness of the body. But he saw something else, too."[2] What did Smith see? Many veterinarians had inspected the horse. "They were only lukewarm about his prospects, eyeing that iffy left foreleg and pronouncing the horse only serviceably useful."[3] Despite all the experts' pronouncements on Seabiscuit's lack of value, Smith urged Howard to buy the horse.

> Everyone was wondering what Smith possibly could have been thinking. The horse was a train wreck. He paced in his stall incessantly. He broke into a lather at the sight of a saddle. He was two hundred pounds underweight and chronically tired. He was so thin, said one observer, that his hips could have made a passable hat rack, but he refused to eat. And that left foreleg didn't look good.[4]

What did Smith see that no one else could see? He could "see the unseen." He looked past Seabiscuit's beat-up body, small size, crooked legs, and wheezy breathing. Smith saw beneath the surface and saw Seabiscuit's heart. He looked into Seabiscuit's eyes and knew he was looking at a great horse. Later, Howard would say, "We had to rebuild him, both mentally and physically, but you don't have to rebuild the heart when it's already there, big as all outdoors."[5] The rest, as they say, is history. Seabiscuit went on to win many races, including the famed, head-to-head, 1938 race at Pimlico against War Admiral and was voted American horse of the year for 1938.[6] Because Smith could see the unseen, he purchased a horse (which everyone else had long since turned their backs on) that went on to become one of the greatest horses in racing history.

Many years ago, my wife, Cheryl, demonstrated her ability to see the unseen one warm summer Friday evening. On that particular evening, we attended an auction where the entire contents of a huge house were being sold. We had attended several of those on-site house auctions before and knew that this auctioneer usually walked around from one location to another where items had been scattered around on the lawn. Because of this, I reasoned we wouldn't need our lawn chairs and, therefore, left them in the trunk of the car. We arrived at the site of the auction only a few minutes before it was to start, so were unable to wander around and pre-examine the items to be sold. We also noticed that, instead of scattered all over the lawn, many of the items that were to be auctioned were in one general location, so while Cheryl stayed for the start of the auction, I walked back down the road a few hundred feet to the car to retrieve our lawn chairs.

I was gone only a few minutes, but upon returning, I found Cheryl waiting for me with a big grin on her face. "I got it for only ten dollars," she excitedly announced to me. Cautiously, I asked, "What did you buy?"

She pointed to the ugliest bright orange dining room buffet I had ever seen and replied, "That."

"You can't be serious!" I moaned. "I wouldn't want to haul that thing home even if you had gotten it for free!" Despite my protests, at the end of the auction, we handed over our ten-dollar bill, placed the buffet in the trailer, drove home, and found a spot for it in the garage. After Cheryl stripped it and I refinished it, the piece was beautiful and it became a part of our dining room furniture for over thirty years. Why did Cheryl and I see a very different buffet that beautiful Friday evening? Cheryl *could see the unseen.* I saw the ugly, orange-painted buffet; she saw the beautiful, yet still hidden, wood beneath the paint. Seeing the unseen drew Cheryl to inexpensively purchase a beautiful dining room buffet.

For me, one of the best illustrations that helps me understand the concept of "seeing the unseen" are the "Magic Eye" pictures, the 3D stereograms, which were so popular in the late 1980s and early 1990s. During the height of their popularity, they could be seen prominently displayed nearly everywhere we looked. Entire books were devoted to pictures of them, and calendars were created with a different stereogram for each month. On the surface, each stereogram was merely a multi-colored geometric design. We had to train our eyes to look deeper, beyond the geometric design, to see the unseen picture *hidden beneath the surface.* It took practice and skill to learn to see the unseen, but when it came into focus, we were overjoyed.

Learning to see the unseen is essential to a vital, healthy, growing, spiritual life. Although our cornea, lens, retina, and optic nerve can clearly visualize the physical world around us, the unseen spiritual world must be seen with the eyes of our hearts. Because the spiritual world is invisible to our physical eyes, it is tempting to ignore it and to declare it as nonexistent; or if we concede to its existence, we dismiss it as of very little importance.

The apostle Paul, however, disagrees. He says it this way, "So we fix our eyes not on what is seen, but on what is unseen. For what is seen is temporary, but what is unseen is eternal" (2 Cor. 4:18).

How can we fix our eyes on the unseen? After all, the unseen is, well, unseen—it is not visible to the human eye. Jesus tried (unsuccessfully, at times) to teach His disciples to see the unseen world. He told them stories—called parables—that they could easily understand and visualize with their *physical* eyes, but had difficulty understanding and visualizing with their *spiritual* eyes.

In one parable, Jesus talked about different types of soils, seeds, and the farmer who sowed them. By Him telling biblical truths in story-form, we learn about ancient farming, but we also learn how to train our eyes to see beneath the physical realities of the story and see the lesson that Jesus is teaching. When Jesus talked about hidden treasure found in a field, a sheep that was lost, or a loving father who ran to meet his wayward son, we can train our eyes to see beneath the physical stories to see the more important spiritual truths. These are truths that must be seen with the eyes of our hearts.

Jesus also used metaphors when He taught. When He said that *He is the vine and we are the branches*, we must train our hearts' eyes to see beneath literal vines and branches and see the spiritual realities of which He speaks. When He said He is a door, the light of the world, the bread of life, living water, or the Good Shepherd, we know what He means if we look past the physical and see through the eyes of our hearts. In order to understand Jesus' parables and metaphors, we must see past the obvious, physically visible, earthly stories and see the vastly more important spiritual stories Jesus wants to teach us. When we do, we see with the eyes of our hearts; we see the unseen.

When we read Jesus' stories and metaphors multiple times and they become familiar to us, we learn to interpret and understand what Jesus is teaching us. This is very good and important, but we must also learn how to transfer that skill to interpret the experiences in our daily lives. If we lack that skill, and therefore cannot see effectively with the eyes of our hearts, we will very often become confused and misinterpret much of our lives. This misinterpretation will occur most often during our difficult and challenging times— just when we most need clarity. Without that clarity, without that ability to see the unseen, we easily lose heart and become bewildered, fearful, angry, anxious, or discouraged.

There are many biblical examples of people who experienced this. One of my favorite Old Testament stories can be found in the Second Book of Kings, chapter six. The nations of Israel and Aram were at war. Whenever the king of Aram attempted to ambush Israel, God revealed the king's plans and the location of the attack to Elisha, who then relayed the information to the king of Israel. After several frustrated ambush attempts, the king of Aram began to suspect a traitor in his ranks, but one of his officers reassured him that a traitor was not the culprit. He said, "Elisha, the prophet who is in Israel, tells the king of Israel the very words you speak in your bedroom" (6:12b). The king then commanded his officer to, "Go, find out where he is ... so I can send men and capture him" (6:13a). When the king found out that Elijah was in Dothan, "he sent horses and chariots and a strong force there. They went by night and surrounded the city" (6:14).

The Aramean army arrived at night and surrounded the city of Dothan, where Elisha and his servant were staying. In the morning, upon awakening, Elisha's servant went out for a stroll on the city walls. Much to his fear and dismay, he was shocked to see the multitude of Aramean horses and chariots surrounding the city. The servant rushed back to Elisha's room only to find him calm, confident, and unconcerned.

> *"Oh, my lord, what shall we do?" the servant asked.*
> *"Don't be afraid," the prophet answered. "Those who*
> *are with us are more than those who are with them."*
> *And Elisha prayed, "O LORD, open his eyes so he may*
> *see." Then the LORD opened the servant's eyes, and*
> *he looked and saw the hills full of horses and chariots*
> *of fire all around Elisha.*
>
> *2 Kings 6:15-17*

What a difference it must have made in the servant's heart when he saw the hills filled with horses and chariots of fire. His interpretation of his fearful situation totally changed when he could see the unseen. We need to place ourselves in the servant's sandals and allow ourselves to feel what he must have been feeling in order to understand this story.

How would he have felt upon seeing that massive army surrounding, and ready to invade, the city of Dothan and knowing it meant his most certain death? Perhaps he had tense neck muscles, a headache, a tight knot in the pit of his stomach, heartburn, and a major dose of adrenaline flowing through his body. What happened to all those emotions when his eyes saw the heavenly army of fire? I'm sure that his fear turned to peace, anxiety turned to trust, and uncertainty turned to confidence. His outlook, and the interpretation of his stressful situation, must have dramatically changed when he saw the true picture in all its fullness—when he saw not only the seen world, but also the unseen.

There is a likewise poignant story in the New Testament in the twenty-fourth chapter of the Gospel according to Luke. The story occurs on Sunday afternoon on the road between Jerusalem and Emmaus and involves two of Jesus' followers, who are grieving and very dejected. Jesus was tortured, died by crucifixion, and was buried Friday afternoon. "We had hoped that he was the one who was going to redeem Israel" (Luke 24:21), they moan to the unknown stranger who is walking along with them. In the midst of their grief and dejection, they are also very confused. They know Jesus was killed and buried on Friday, but now today, Sunday, some of the women who also followed Jesus reported that the body was missing from the tomb, and they had seen Jesus alive.

Although the two disciples did not recognize Him, the man walking along-side of them was Jesus. He encouraged the disciples, "And beginning with Moses and all the Prophets, he [Jesus] explained to them what was said in all the Scriptures concerning himself" (Luke 24:27). Upon arriving at Emmaus, the two disciples invited Jesus into their house for the night.

> *When he was at the table with them, he took bread, gave thanks, broke it and began to give it to them. Then their eyes were opened and they recognized him, and he disappeared from their sight. They asked each other, "Were not our hearts burning within us while he talked with us on the road and opened the Scriptures to us?" They got up and returned at once to Jerusalem. There they found the Eleven and those with them, assembled together and saying, "It is true! The Lord has risen and has appeared to Simon." Then the two told what had happened on the way, and how Jesus was recognized by them when he broke the bread.*
>
> *Luke 24:30-35*

Their "burning hearts" were the clue to eyes that were beginning to see the unseen but were still blind. The opening of their eyes turned their emotions 180 degrees from deep sorrow and dejection to unspeakable joy. Again, put yourself in their place. How are you feeling and what difference does "seeing" make in how you view your painful circumstances?

As with Elisha's servant and Jesus' two disciples, we cannot properly understand our situation and our circumstances either if we do not learn to see with the eyes of our hearts. It is the Holy Spirit who opens our eyes, but we also have a responsibility to train the eyes of our hearts to see. The writer of Hebrews says, "Now faith is being sure of what we hope for and certain of what we do not see" (Heb. 11:1). Our walk with Jesus is a walk of faith. We place our faith in that which we cannot see with our physical eyes, but that does not make those things less real. The Holy Spirit helps us see the unseen and it gives us hope. The writer of Hebrews also tells us that Moses "persevered because he saw him who is invisible" (Heb. 11:27). We also can persevere in the hard times of our lives because we have learned to see Him who is invisible.

The apostle Paul prayed that God would turn on the light switch in the hearts of the Ephesian believers so they could see. "I pray also that the eyes of your heart may be enlightened in order that you may know the hope to which he has called you, the riches of his glorious inheritance in the saints, and his incomparably great power for us who believe" (Eph. 1: 18-19a). If we are to follow Jesus and rightly interpret our lives, we must know the hope, riches, and power that are ours through Jesus Christ, our Lord. Knowing them and living them necessitate heart eyes that can see.

Seeing the unseen will change how we view our lives and how we live our lives. It will help us navigate through calm as well as treacherous waters. But how do we learn to see beneath the surface of our lives? That is what this book is intending to show us. I invite you, the reader, to take this journey with me.[7]

Each chapter can stand alone; so, although I have given some thought to the order in which they were placed, they can be read in any order desired. If there is a particular topic that is of more interest to you, read that chapter first. My prayer is that by the end of this book, we each can more clearly understand, follow, love, and see the One who deeply loves us and who desires an intimate relationship with us.

As Frederick Buechner said, "To love God means to *pay attention*, be mindful, be open to the possibility that God is with you in ways that, unless you have your eyes open, you may never glimpse. He speaks words that, unless you have your ears open, you may never hear."[8]

I

Remembering God's Acts of Grace

Although we love God, obeying, following, serving, and staying close to Him are not always easy. It's tempting to slowly wander off course as we avail ourselves of all the world has to offer, even when many of those things injure our hearts and negatively impact our relationship with Him. In addition, during the difficult times in our lives, doubts concerning the reliability and sincerity of God's love and care for us and doubts concerning His continual presence with us find a way of creeping into our minds and hearts.

God is fully aware of this when, through Moses, He speaks to the nation of Israel on the eve of their invasion into the Promised Land. When the "going gets tough," what is it that will help them not get discouraged and help them not doubt God's love, care, and continual presence? When they enter the new land, what will keep them from succumbing to all the temptations that are about to flood over them as they encounter a new culture with many attractive, though temporary, pleasures that will cause them to stray from the life God has laid out for them?

What does Moses tell them? "Only be careful, and watch yourselves closely so that you do not forget the things your eyes have seen or let them fade from your heart as long as you live. Teach them to your children and to their children after them" (Deut. 4:9).

The people entering the land had seen God intervene on their behalf numerous times. In addition to their own personal experiences, their parents, although dead at that time, had witnessed God rescue them from slavery in Egypt, had watched Him part the Red Sea so they could all walk across on dry ground, and had watched as the pursuing Egyptian army was drowned when the Red Sea closed back on them. They must have heard their parents and grandparents tell the stories over and over again until they, themselves, could "see" those miraculous deeds from the hands of a powerful and loving God.

In essence, Moses told them, *Watch, and stay alert. Be careful. It's going to be easy to forget everything that God has done for you, but don't forget. Your very lives depend on remembering. Your relationship with God depends on remembering. Your ability to not get discouraged when trials come your way depends on remembering. Be encouraged as you remember the miracles God has performed on your behalf. God has never forsaken you and He never will. No matter how difficult your circumstances appear to you, know that God is with you, and remember what He has done for you in the past. Don't get drawn into worshiping the gods of your new neighbors. Remember the covenant you made with God. Remember He loves you and has chosen you as His people. Follow Him, obey Him, and remember how He has led you in the past. Whatever you do, do not forget.*

Moses wanted them to be vigilant. He knew they would not *suddenly* forget what God had done for them. He knew they would easily remember God's miracles and the evidences of His grace and mercy, "just as though they had happened yesterday" for days or weeks, or perhaps months. But if they did not *intentionally* remind themselves, if they did not continually refresh their memories, those memories would fade.

Memories can fade so slowly that we are not even aware we are forgetting.

Memories will fade like a beautiful picture, once painted with brilliant colors, fades as it hangs year after year on the wall of my sun porch. From one year to the next, I do not notice any change in the vibrancy of the colors until one day, I look at it with fresh eyes, and the muted, faded colors startle me. Memories will fade like the ink on the pages of old love letters, stored for decades in a hot attic. Memories will fade like a once close friendship fades when it is left unattended—when getting together now feels strained and awkward. Fading is gradual. We don't often notice things that fade until it is too late.

That was what Moses was trying to tell them. In essence he said, *Folks, you must remember; you must frequently rehearse your promises to God and rehearse His many acts of grace. You must keep your memory fresh. You must tell the stories out loud. You must surround yourselves with visible reminders so you do not forget.*

Moses continued his thoughts:

> *These commandments that I give you today are to be on your hearts. Impress them on your children. Talk about them when you sit at home and when you walk along the road, when you lie down and when you get up. Tie them as symbols on your hands and bind them on your foreheads. Write them on the doorframes of your houses and on your gates. When the LORD your God brings you into the land he swore to your fathers, to Abraham, Isaac and Jacob, to give you—a land with large, flourishing cities you did not build, houses filled with all kinds of good things you did not provide, wells you did not dig, and vineyards and olive groves you did not plant—then when you eat and are satisfied, be careful that you do not forget*

> *the* LORD, *who brought you out of Egypt, out of the*
> *land of slavery.*
>
> *Deuteronomy 6:6-12*

Forgetting is effortless when we don't continually rehearse what God has done for us. If we are to remember God's acts of grace, we must learn them, meditate on them, teach them, surround ourselves with visual reminder symbols and, above all, pass them along to the next generation.

How did the nation of Israel fare once they entered the Promised Land? Did they heed Moses' warnings and admonitions? "After that whole generation had been gathered to their ancestors, another generation grew up who knew neither the LORD nor what he had done for Israel" (Judg. 2:10).

What?! *One* generation? How is that even possible? Judges 2:10 is one of the most tragic verses in the Bible. How could memories have faded to oblivion in just one generation? Read through the Old Testament Book of Judges to learn the result of their faded memories. "In those days Israel had no king; everyone did as he saw fit" (Judg. 17:6). So sad. As we continue to read through the book of Judges, we see that although they would occasionally rally, they quickly reverted back to forgetfulness and, each time they did, they once again drifted away from God and His ways—as do we, if we too, forget.

How can we change this trend? How can the colors of our memories remain deep and vibrant? What can we do that will help us remember? As previously mentioned, left to its natural course, memory will slowly fade. When harmful pleasures tempt us and lure us away from God's way of true physical, emotional, and spiritual health, or when we are drawn to doubt God's goodness during times of suffering, our hearts and minds must remember. Memories of God's acts of grace in our lives, if long neglected, will rarely surface during difficult times or times of temptation. How do we keep our memories of God's goodness and His acts of grace fresh in our minds? We must be intentional. We must have a plan to remember, and we must work at that plan every day of our lives. We can each come up with ideas on how to keep our memories fresh year after year and generation after generation.

First, like King David, we can talk to our inmost being. David regularly talked to his soul and reminded himself not to forget.

> *Praise the* LORD, *my soul; all my inmost being, praise his holy name. Praise the* LORD, *my soul, and forget not all his benefits—who forgives all your sins and heals all your diseases, who redeems your life from the pit and crowns you with love and compassion, who satisfies your desires with good things so that your youth is renewed like the eagle's.*
>
> *Psalm 103:1-5*

Second, when painful events tempt us to lose heart, we, like the psalmist Asaph, can cry out to God for help. While groaning and weeping and wondering if God would ever again pour out His blessing on him, Asaph questioned,

> *Will the Lord reject forever? Will he never show his favor again? Has his unfailing love vanished forever? Has his promise failed for all time? Has God forgotten to be merciful? Has he in anger withheld his compassion?*
>
> *Psalm 77:7-9*

But while waiting on God, his eyes were opened and his view of life and his perspective on the situation changed. What happened?

What turned the tide? What made the difference? In God's presence, he remembered.

> *Then I thought, "To this I will appeal: the years*
> *when the Most High stretched out his right hand.*
> *I will remember the deeds of the* LORD; *yes, I will*
> *remember your miracles of long ago. I will consider*
> *all your works and meditate on all your mighty deeds."*
> *Your ways, God, are holy. What god is as great as our*
> *God? You are the God who performs miracles; you*
> *display your power among the peoples. With your*
> *mighty arm you redeemed your people, the descen-*
> *dants of Jacob and Joseph.*
>
> *Psalm 77:10-15*

Third, we need to meet regularly with other believers and remember, together, God's greatest act of grace. God sent His Son, Jesus, to earth to become human—like each of us. The Creator became the Created. He came into the world as a baby, lived, died, and was buried, then He rose back to life. He died that we might have life. Jesus used the Passover supper—that great time of remembering how God rescued the nation of Israel from slavery in Egypt— as a time to remember a new rescue, a new salvation from slavery. This new rescue was not from slavery to the Egyptian Pharaoh but from slavery to the power and penalty of sin. This new rescue occurred when Jesus shed His blood while nailed to a wooden cross erected on a hill outside of Jerusalem.

At that last Passover supper with His disciples, "he [Jesus] took bread, gave thanks and broke it, and gave it to them [His disciples], saying, 'This is my body given for you; do this in remembrance of me'" (Luke 22:19). Jesus took the third cup of wine, which was normally used in the Passover meal and said, "This cup is the new covenant in my blood, which is poured out for you" (Luke 22:20). Jesus used the cup of wine to symbolize His blood that was soon to be shed, and He used the bread to symbolize His body that was soon to be broken. Jesus told them to do this so they would not forget His death. He said, *Remember what I have done for you. Don't ever forget. Use this Passover bread and wine to remember me, to remember my sacrifice, and to remember my suffering for you.*

The apostle Paul said it this way,

> *For I received from the Lord what I also passed on to you: The Lord Jesus, on the night he was betrayed, took bread, and when he had given thanks, he broke it and said, "This is my body, which is for you; do this in remembrance of me." In the same way, after supper he took the cup, saying, "This cup is the new covenant in my blood; do this, whenever you drink it, in remembrance of me." For whenever you eat this bread and drink this cup, you proclaim the Lord's death until he comes.*
>
> *1 Corinthians 11:23-26*

David E. Garland states that the Greek word that is here translated as "remembrance" is not merely meant as a time to remind ourselves of Jesus' death like we might "read an inscription on a tombstone." We don't simply say, *Oh, yes, He died for me, I know that*, then get up and leave the room and go about our business as usual. True remembrance leads us to *relive* Jesus' death as we become totally present to the horror of Jesus' sacrifice, pain, and death. His death becomes so real to us that our time of remembrance leads us to worship, and our worship leads us to obedience. Authentic remembrance impacts our behavior.[1] Jeffrey D. Arthurs adds, "The proof of memory is fidelity."[2]

Fourth, God encouraged the nation of Israel to use physically visible memory aids, and we can do the same. On the night God freed Israel from slavery, He told them, "This is a day you are to commemorate; for the generations to come you shall celebrate it as a festival to the Lord—a lasting ordinance" (Exod. 12:14). The Passover celebration became a yearly reminder of what God had done for them.

When God provided manna for them to eat in the desert, He said, "Take an omer of manna and keep it for the generations to come, so they can see the bread I gave you to eat in the desert when I brought you out of Egypt" (Exod. 16:32).

As a daily reminder of His commands,

> *The LORD said to Moses, "Speak to the Israelites and say to them: Throughout the generations to come you are to make tassels on the corners of your garments, with a blue cord on each tassel. You will have these tassels to look at and so you will remember all the commands of the LORD, that you may obey them and not prostitute yourselves by chasing after the lusts of your own hearts and eyes. Then you will remember to obey all my commands and will be consecrated to your God. I am the LORD your God, who brought you out of Egypt to be your God. I am the LORD your God."*
>
> *Numbers 15:37-41*

The ram's horn known as the shofar, "has been the trumpet that has called God's people to repentance, faith and devotion."[3] Every time the ram's horn is blown, it reminds the people of the ram, caught in the thicket, that Abraham found and used as a substitute sacrifice in place of his son, Isaac.[4]

The seven-branched candlestick or lampstand known as the menorah was a piece of tabernacle furniture used to provide light in the Holy Place but was also a continual reminder of God's call on His people to be a light to the rest of the world (Isa. 42:6).[5]

While at flood stage, God miraculously stopped the waters of the Jordan River so the nation could cross over into the Promised Land. God did not want the people to forget. This passage relates the story.

> *Joshua called together the twelve men he had appointed from the Israelites, one from each tribe, and said to them, "Go over before the ark of the LORD your God into the middle of the Jordan. Each of you is to take up a stone on his shoulder, according to the number of the tribes of the Israelites, to serve as a sign among you. In the future, when your children ask you, 'What do these stones mean?' tell them that the flow of the Jordan was cut off before the ark of the covenant of the LORD. When it crossed the Jordan, the waters of the Jordan were cut off. These stones are to be a memorial to the people of Israel forever."*
>
> *Joshua 4:4-7*

After a victorious battle against the Philistines, "Samuel took a stone and set it up between Mizpah and Shen. He named it Ebenezer, saying, 'Thus far has the Lord helped us'" (1 Sam. 7:12).

These are just a few examples of how the nation of Israel used physical objects as visual reminders to help them keep their memories fresh so they did not fade away. We, too, can do this. Perhaps the most common object we use to keep our memories of Jesus' death alive is a cross. Churches display them, homes display them, they are used as pendants hung from gold chains for necklaces, they are made into bookmarks, and so on. We could also keep a large, rough-cut nail on our desk to remind us of Jesus' death. We assemble nativity figures around a manger scene during the Christmas season to help us remember the birth of Jesus. Some people take smooth, polished stones and etch into each stone a different attribute of God as a reminder of who He is. If we begin to think about it, we can come up with many ideas for placing objects in frequently viewed locations around our home as reminders of God's grace.

Think of your own unique encounters with God's powerful hand of protection, encouragement, or comfort. What object could you purchase or create as a reminder of that event? Have you been in a serious motor vehicle accident when God protected you from injury? As a reminder, buy a small Matchbox or Hot Wheel car, take a hammer and crush the front end of the car, then take the mangled little car and place it where you will see it often.

Fifth, we could keep a journal of our stories. All of us have stories of times when God amazingly intervened on our behalf, but, unfortunately, we so quickly forget them. However, if we write them down and read them often, we can keep our memories fresh, and they can give us strength and courage when we need to remember them the most.

When I was eighteen years old and a freshman at Houghton College, because I was a poor college student with no money for a bus ticket, I decided to hitchhike from Houghton, NY, down to Roanoke, VA, to see my sister during our Christmas school break. Driving from Houghton to Roanoke was a 485 mile trip, but I determined to hitchhike that distance—in the winter. Since I did not own a winter coat or winter boots, I wore a rather thin jacket and a pair of regular walking shoes. Although hitchhiking was very different in 1968 from what it is today, it still was not an entirely safe practice. There was also the safety concern of standing out in the bitter cold for hours at a time on the side of the road, waiting for a ride while improperly clothed. Amazingly I made it down and back and do not recall being cold, nor do I recall standing on the side of the road for long periods of time waiting for rides.

On the return trip to Houghton College, I was blessed to have a kind young gentleman stop and transport me the final one hundred and fifty miles or so back to my college dorm. I suppose, because we were in the car for several hours together, at some point along the way, he asked me if I wanted to drive. Keep in mind I had just received my driver's license about four months before, I had gotten very little driving practice because I did not own a car, and I had no experience driving in snow or on icy roads. Did any of those factors cause me to decline his offer to drive? Nope! My naïve brain was very confident of my driving skills. In answer to his question, I said, "Sure!" So he pulled to the side of the road, we both got out, switched places and, with me at the wheel, we continued on our journey.

I have no idea how long I'd been driving on the snow-packed road when I approached a rather steep incline with no visibility beyond the crest of the hill. I do not remember how fast I was driving, but I do remember I was not driving slowly. As I crested the hill and began my descent, I was able to see that, in about one hundred yards, the road ended in a "T." As I looked ahead, I could see I was rapidly approaching a steel guardrail stretched out directly in front of me, and I could see a solitary man, swinging a flashlight, walking slowly from left to right in front of the guardrail. The route sign on the side of the road directed me to turn left at the "T" and, soon thereafter, a stop sign reminded me to come to a complete stop before making my turn.

Allowing for plenty of stopping distance, I removed my right foot from the accelerator and pressed firmly on the brake pedal. Absolutely nothing happened; there was not one iota of speed reduction. My brain instantly shifted into high alert mode and I responded by pressing ever more firmly on the brake pedal. *Nothing.* We were swiftly approaching the guardrail—and the man who was now directly in front of the car. I continued to press as firmly as I could on the brake pedal (pumping the brakes, what's that?), but now I also turned the steering wheel as far as it would turn to the left. Still nothing. We continued to barrel straight ahead, speed entirely unchecked. I can still see the stark panic in the man's eyes. At that point, he still had plenty of time to run and get out of my way and avoid being crushed between the car and the guardrail. However, being unsure of which direction to run, he did not move. There he remained, directly in the path of our oncoming car, frozen in my headlights—dancing. Yes, dancing!

Picture a scene in an old western movie when, threatening a scared townsman, a gunslinger commands him to dance. The man begins to dance with his feet going every which way to avoid the bullets at his feet. Can you picture the scene? Well, that's exactly what that frightened man was doing on the snow-packed road up ahead of us while our car rolled ever closer.

Meanwhile, there I was, in the car, very wide awake, beginning to panic, holding tightly to the steering wheel that was turned sharply to the left, right foot jammed down on the brake as hard as my leg could push, flying straight ahead, totally unchecked, ever and ever closer to crushing the man between our car and the guardrail, totaling the car, and severely injuring (or killing) my passenger and me. Suddenly, inexplicably, without conscious thought or intention on my part, I was surprised to discover I had lifted my foot from the brake pedal. The result? The car, without slipping or sliding, instantly, and incredibly smoothly, turned left and slowly came to a stop a few feet down the road.

In a quiet but strong and tense voice, the owner of the car ordered, "Pull over to the side of the road. Where did you get your license, from Sears?" We switched places and then rode on in stony silence for what seemed like an hour—but I'm sure was only a few minutes—until he began to talk again and told me it wasn't my fault (It largely *was* my fault!) because the road was unusually slippery. As we got closer to Houghton, he amazingly and graciously drove many miles out of his way to deliver me right to the college campus.

What caused me to suddenly lift my foot from the pedal at the perfect spot on the road to effect a smooth left turn and not slide off the road? Although it had made no difference in the speed of the car, my brain and every nerve and muscle in my body were engaged in the strategy of maintaining unrelenting pressure on the brake pedal. Nothing could have induced me to lift my foot. Nothing. So, why did I? Coincidence? Good luck? Happenstance? Chance? My leg got tired of pressing? Maybe, but for me, the driver of the car who lived through it, I am totally convinced it was divine intervention.

To this day, there is no question in my mind or heart that God sent an angel who grabbed my knee and pulled up on my leg, thereby completely disengaging my foot from the surface of the pedal. God was gracious to me and sent me aid. Remembering this story in the midst of a trial in my life helps give me perspective.

It reminds me that God is good and loving. It reminds me I am never alone. It reminds me God cared for me on that snow-packed road in the dark of night and I can be assured He will care for me again in my present trial. (Following through with the above mentioned visible objects as reminder aids, I could create a small snowy diorama with a road coming to a "T" and a guardrail at the end of the road. I could insert a small figure on the road in front of the guardrail and a small Matchbox car on the road. Setting it on my desk would remind me to relive the event each time I look at it.)

To remember a story like this one is not merely to say to myself, "Oh, yes, I remember that." True remembering means we *relive* the story. We take the time to sit down and pause; we allow our mind, heart, emotions, thoughts, and memories to transport us back in time to the event, where, step by step, we relive it. We allow our-selves the time to see it, hear it, and feel it. As mentioned earlier, in the Bible, the Greek word translated as "remember" means much more than simple passive recall; it is an active word. True remem-bering should change our lives in significant ways and lead us to action, prayer, belief, or confession.[6] In other words, it will power-fully impact how we live.

Ian Pitt-Watson states, "Remembering is far more than recall. When you remember something, if done right, what was present before becomes present once again."[7] Robert Cosand says, "Remembrance is an understanding of the reality of the past in such a way that the events of the past become a force in the present, pro-ducing some activity of will or of body or both."[8]

There is a great illustration of this principle at work in the Old Testament book of 1 Samuel. The result of true remembering leads to perhaps one of the best known stories in the Bible.

When Saul was king of Israel and David was still a shepherd tending his father's sheep, David travelled to his brothers who were soldiers in Israel's army, which was engaged in war with the Philistines. David arrived at the army camp just as all the soldiers were mobilizing to take their battle positions. As David watched, the nine-foot tall giant Goliath stepped out from the Philistine line and began to shout at the Israeli army, taunting them to send a soldier over to engage in hand-to-hand combat. All the while Goliath was shouting and taunting, he was trash-talking the army of God. David was shocked that there was not one soldier willing to step up and take on the challenge, so he strode over to King Saul and declared,

> *"Let no one lose heart on account of this Philistine;*
> *your servant will go and fight him." Saul replied,*
> *"You are not able to go out against this Philistine*

and fight him; you are only a boy, and he has been a fighting man from his youth." But David said to Saul, "your servant has been keeping his father's sheep. When a lion or a bear came and carried off a sheep from the flock, I went after it, and struck it and rescued the sheep from its mouth. When it turned on me, I seized it by its hair, struck it and killed it. Your servant has killed both the lion and the bear; this uncircumcised Philistine will be like one of them, because he has defied the armies of the living God. The Lord who delivered me from the paw of the lion and the paw of the bear will deliver me from the hand of this Philistine."

1 Samuel 17:32-37

David said to King Saul, *Don't lose heart, I'll fight Goliath.* Then David *remembered.* Aloud, he told his story to the king. He did not just recall, but he relived the stories of how God demonstrated His power through him to kill the bear and the lion. David continued, *Saul, this is no different. God will demonstrate His power through me today as He did in the past.* David remembered God's previous acts of grace and it gave him confidence, courage, and strength for his present.

Similarly, remembering our past, and how God worked on our behalf, can also give us confidence, courage, and strength to face our present difficulties. We need to write our stories, read them frequently, and allow them to remind us of the truth of God's love, mercy, and grace.

2

Enriching Our Understanding of God Through Metaphors

Many of us would agree with biblical writers when they lament that it is, at times, challenging to comprehend God's motives, purposes, priorities, values, desires, and the decisions He makes.

In Elihu's feeble attempt to comfort Job and assist him in making some sense of his unthinkable pain, grief, and suffering, he proclaims, "How great is God—beyond our understanding!" (Job 36:26). Centuries later, in the midst of difficult times, the nation of Israel is convinced God has forsaken them. They complain, "My way is hidden from the Lord; my cause is disregarded by my God" (Isa. 40:27). The prophet Isaiah helps them see beneath the surface of their present situation by reminding them of God's greatness. He asks them why they are complaining, shakes his head in disbelief, challenges their thinking, and says, "Do you not know? Have you not heard? The Lord is the everlasting God, the Creator of the ends of the earth. He will not grow tired or weary, and His understanding no one can fathom" (Isa. 40:28). On another occasion, Isaiah quotes God: "'For my thoughts are not your thoughts, neither are your ways my ways,' declares the Lord. 'As the heavens are higher than the earth, so are my ways higher than your ways and my thoughts than your thoughts'" (Isa. 55:8-9).

David agrees when, in worship, he humbly affirms, "Great is the Lord and most worthy of praise; his greatness no one can fathom" (Ps. 145:3). Or, as another translation reads, "his greatness is unsearchable" (ESV). No ocean floor can be found when we attempt to sound the depths of God's understanding or greatness. God's ways and thoughts are beyond comprehension.

In awe and amazement, the apostle Paul sings a hymn of praise to God. "Oh, the depth of the riches of the wisdom and knowledge of God! How unsearchable his judgments, and his paths beyond tracing out! Who has known the mind of the Lord? Or who has been his counselor?" (Rom. 11:33-34). God's judgments are unsearchable—beyond our ability to understand—and His paths are untraceable.[1] We cannot trace or track God's footprints as He walks from eternity past to eternity future.

Commenting on this conundrum, Brennan Manning writes, "Although God has revealed Himself in creation and in history, the surest way to know God is, in the words of Thomas Aquinas, as *tamquam ignotum*, as utterly unknowable. No thought can contain Him, no word can express Him, He is beyond anything we can intellectualize or imagine."[2]

If all of this is true (and it is!), and God is beyond our understanding (and He is!), is there any hope for truly knowing Him? Can we, with our limited knowledge and language, describe and relate to a God who is so far above anything we can ever envision? Is it possible to convey in words the nature and attributes of a God who is indescribable? The biblical writers do their best but, for the most part, must resign themselves to using metaphors to describe God and the nature of the relationship He desires to develop with us. These metaphors are never perfect—they are only a shadow of the real thing—but they help us more clearly see facets of God that otherwise could be complex or confusing.

Metaphors are *word pictures*. Pictures can be valuable tools in helping us make sense of concepts that are difficult to understand or explain. As the old saying goes, "One picture is worth a thousand words." A character in Ivan Turgenev's 1862 novel *Fathers and Sons*, says, "A picture shows me at a glance what would take up all of ten pages in a book."[3]

Metaphors are "a figure of speech in which a word or phrase literally denoting one kind of object or idea is used in place of another to suggest a likeness or analogy between them."[4] Although they only hint at reality and are an imperfect, faint depiction or a mere shadow of that which they attempt to represent, they enhance and enrich our comprehension, give us a visual description of a confusing word, and/or add color to an otherwise drab description of an object, person, or event. Some well-known examples of metaphors are: "He has a heart of stone," "I'm dead tired," and "My memory is a little foggy."

No one metaphor can remotely capture the essence of God. Each metaphor is like a single facet of a diamond or a single piece of a puzzle that, only when combined with multiple other metaphors, can begin to give us a meager glimpse of the full picture of the character, nature, and attributes of this God we have come to love. There are multiple metaphors for God seen throughout the pages of the Bible, but we will limit ourselves to exploring only five.

God as a Strong Tower

Solomon states, "The name of the Lord is a strong tower; the righteous run to it and are safe" (Prov. 18:10). How does an image of a strong tower enhance our understanding of God? In ancient Israel, towers were built for defensive military purposes and were incorporated into a city wall or built as a separate structure on a hill to function as a watchtower. Some watchtowers were like small fortresses and were used to guard major roads or large vineyards. In some cases, villages grew up around these previously existing watchtowers. These watchtowers then served to protect not only the road or vineyard but also the villagers.[5]

While touring Jerusalem during our recent trip to Israel, our guide drew our attention to the towers built into the city walls and pointed out for us that they were taller than the wall and jutted out several feet beyond the wall. He said this served to give the archers a clear sightline along the entire height and length of the wall and greatly increased their ability to defend the city should an invasion attempt occur. These towers were placed on each side of the city gates and at multiple other strategic locations along the wall, such as at corners or sharp curves.

By using this metaphor, Solomon is encouraging us to run to God for protection. This act is a demonstration of the faith we place in an all-powerful and eternal God. His name reveals His character and attributes. We can run to God and know we will be safe because of who God is. God reveals His name to Moses as, "I AM WHO I AM" in other words, *I will be what I will be* (Exod. 3:14). And later, He again tells Moses, "I am the LORD" (Exod. 6:2), or, in Hebrew, "YHWH" (now written and pronounced "Yahweh"). The chief meaning of this name has to do with His existence. "He is the One who was, who is, and who always will be."[6] He is eternal. He never had a beginning and He will never have an end. While giving Moses the two stone tablets on Mount Sinai, God further defines His name,

The Lord, the Lord, the compassionate and gracious God, slow to anger, abounding in love and faithfulness, maintaining love to thousands, and forgiving

wickedness, rebellion and sin. Yet He does not leave the guilty unpunished; He punishes the children and their children for the sin of the fathers to the third and fourth generation.

Exodus 34:6-7

The entire Bible further defines God's character and attributes, all of which reassure us we can depend upon His name for protection. YHWH keeps us safe and secure from all that would attempt to injure, defeat, or destroy us. The word "safe" literally means "high," or to be "set on high," or "safely on high."[7] The International Standard Version of the Bible translates this verse as, "The name of the LORD is a strong tower; a righteous person rushes to it and is lifted up above the danger." As we run to God for safety and security, He lifts us up high into His protective tower.

David declares, "Hear my cry, O God; listen to my prayer. From the ends of the earth I call to you, I call as my heart grows faint; lead me to the rock that is higher than I. For you have been my refuge, a strong tower against the foe" (Ps. 61:1-3). David uses this metaphor to describe his own personal experience of how God has been his refuge and has protected him from his enemies by lifting him high to safety.

God will also be a strong tower for us, but we must understand this does not mean He will protect us from all physical harm. Look through the stories of the Bible. Was God a strong tower for Jacob's favorite son, Joseph? Was God a strong tower for the apostle Paul, or for Stephen, or for Peter? Each one of them endured great suffering and trials. However, as we view their lives, knowing the end of the story, we can confirm that God was unquestionably a strong tower to each one of them—and will be for us as well. It is not always easy to know how to pray and then trust God to be our tower during those difficult times. As Ruth Haley Barton asks, "What is the use of praying if at the very moment of prayer, we have so little confidence in God that we are busy planning our own kind of answer to our prayer?"[8] Trusting God is not always easy, but He will always answer our prayers and protect us in His time and in His way.

God as a Spring of Living Water

Although water is a critically essential component for sustaining life, for those of us in affluent regions of the world, it is so readily available we take it for granted and hardly give it a second thought. In fact, water is so plentiful that many refuse to drink the water from their faucets if they judge its taste to be even slightly disagreeable. These people will spend hundreds of dollars a year buying bottled water because it is, for various reasons, perceived to be more palatable, sanitary, or healthy. In many parts of the world, however, water is very scarce and, even when available, can be contaminated and sicken those who perhaps have walked miles to obtain it.

In ancient Palestine, water was also scarce. To live close to a natural spring was a luxury most Palestinians did not enjoy. While touring Israel, it was amazing to experience the sharp contrast between the miles and miles of desert and the occasional small strip of lush vegetation surrounding a spring, such as the one we encountered at En Gedi. Because digging wells was time-consuming and very costly, and most of the streams and rivers were small and some of them would completely dry up in the summer, much of their water was obtained from rainwater. Unfortunately, even rainwater was in short supply during the summer; therefore, it was collected (from roof and street run-off) in large cisterns and saved for times of drought. We viewed and actually climbed down into several of the mammoth cisterns that were dug and lined with waterproof plaster. Some cisterns were deeper than one hundred feet and one of the cisterns beneath the temple area in Jerusalem could hold between two and three million gallons of water.[9] Although much care was given to preserving the precious water, the plaster could crack, the cisterns leak, and valuable water lost. Water that did not leak out could remain in the cisterns for long periods of time, become stagnant, grow bacteria (remember, some of it came from street run-off), absorb minerals from the earth, and become unpleasant or unhealthy to drink. Very few people in ancient Palestine took water—of any quality—for granted. To obtain clean, fresh, cold water directly from a natural spring was an extravagance many only dreamed about. Within this context, God's use of *a spring of living water* to describe Himself must have been quickly comprehended by those listening to Jeremiah.

God explains, "My people have committed two sins: They have forsaken me, the spring of living water, and have dug their own cisterns, broken cisterns that cannot hold water" (Jer. 2:13). God, through Jeremiah described how His people have rejected Him—a continuous flow of fresh, clean, cold, life-giving water—to worship other gods that He likens to leaky cisterns. Unlike us, these people knew exactly what God was talking about and could clearly imagine the difference between stagnant "dead" cistern water and "living" fresh spring water.

Jeremiah also uses this metaphor, "O Lord, the hope of Israel, all who forsake you will be put to shame. Those who turn away from you will be written in the dust because they have forsaken the Lord, the spring of living water" (Jer. 17:13). In order to truly understand this insightful word picture we must look through the eyes of the Israelites during Jeremiah's time. This picture helps us appreciate what it means to turn away from following, trusting, and worshipping God—the very source of a never-ending stream of soul-rehydrating cold, fresh, clean spring water—to follow the many local "gods" that offer temporary pleasures but never ultimately deliver on their promises.

In referring to Himself during an encounter with a woman at a community well near a Samaritan village, Jesus also used this metaphor. Incredulous that Jesus, a Jewish man, asked her, a Samaritan woman, for a drink of water, Jesus responded. "If you knew the gift of God and who it is that asks you for a drink, you would have asked him and he would have given you living water. ... Everyone who drinks this water will be thirsty again, but whoever drinks the water I give him will never thirst. Indeed, the water I give him will become in him a spring of water welling up to eternal life" (John 4:10, 13-14).

If we could catch just a glimpse of this metaphor as seen through the eyes of those who struggle to obtain water of any quality—let alone a bountiful supply of fresh, cold, running water from a spring gushing out of the side of the mountain—we could begin to see the refreshing, thirst-quenching, life-giving nature of God and not be tempted to search for life, meaning, purpose, satisfaction, and affirmation from anyone or anything else.

GOD AS A CONSUMING FIRE

Why would some biblical authors use "consuming fire" as a metaphor for God? In both the Old Testament Hebrew and the New Testament Greek, "consuming fire" means a fire that utterly consumes and destroys.[10] For some of us, this may generate a picture of a destructive, ruthless, uncompromising, and angry God. The word "consuming" may also bring to mind negative emotions like consuming anger, consuming hatred, or consuming jealousy—emotions that "take over" our mind, heart, time, and energy at the expense of everything else in our lives and, if unrestrained, destroy us and all those around us.

A consuming fire perhaps calls to mind a fire that roars unchecked through acres of a forest or city, leaving nothing but destruction and death in its path.

On October 8, 1871, on the exact same night that the Peshtigo, Wisconsin, wildfire (considered to be the most destructive wildfire in United States history) burned one and a quarter million acres, and fifteen to twenty-five hundred people lost their lives,[11] The Great Chicago Fire burned up over 2000 acres of the city of Chicago and 300 people lost their lives.[12] Is this what God is like? Does God consume and destroy everything in His path? What are we to learn of God's nature through the use of this metaphor? How does this enhance our understanding of God?

In the Bible, fire is often associated with the presence of God.

- Wielded by cherubim, a flaming sword, flashing back and forth, guards the way to the tree of life following the banishment of Adam and Eve from the Garden of Eden (Gen. 3:24).
- Flames of fire engulf a desert bush within which God speaks to Moses (Exod. 3:2-5).
- By night, God leads the Nation of Israel through the desert in a pillar of fire (Exod. 13:21).
- While all God's people stand at the base of Mount Sinai, God descends on the mountain in fire (Exod. 19:18).
- As Moses ascends Mount Sinai, God's glory settles on the mountain, and "To the Israelites the glory of the Lord [appears] like a consuming fire on top of the mountain" (Exod. 24:17).
- During Elijah's contest with the prophets of Baal, God answers Elijah's prayer and sends fire from heaven which consumes his sacrifice, the wood, the stones, the soil, and all the water in the trench (1 Kings 18:20-40).

- On the day of Pentecost flames of fire appear on the heads of the disciples as the Holy Spirit fills them (Acts 2:1-4).

Moses introduces the "consuming fire" metaphor to the Israelites, who are preparing to cross the Jordan River to claim the Promised Land (Deut. 4:24), where they will encounter people who worship multiple gods. In fact, polytheism is the norm for all the nations around that region, but God expects the Nation of Israel—His chosen people—to rid themselves of all idols and exclusively worship Him. Blessings are promised if they obey, and curses are promised if they disobey. God's people are not to be careless or indifferent to His expectations and desires, nor are they to take Him lightly. Since God expects them to faithfully worship Him with respect, fear, awe, and reverence, Moses uses this metaphor to warn the people of God's hatred and intolerance of idolatry and the consequences to all those who refuse to obey. God warns them, saying, "Do not worship any other god, for the Lord, whose name is Jealous, is a jealous God (Exod. 34:14).

The author of the book of Hebrews warns his audience about rejecting God or slowly drifting away from Him. He wants them to have grateful hearts as they remember what God has done for them and is yet to do in the future. Hearts of deep gratitude lead to humble worship marked by reverence and awe (Heb. 12:28).

Now, many centuries later, the author repeats Moses' metaphor to remind the people that, although God is full of love, grace, mercy, and compassion, He is also a consuming fire, expects their full obedience, and will not tolerate a cavalier attitude toward His majesty, holiness, and sovereignty. Earlier in his book, the author of Hebrews states, "It is a dreadful thing to fall into the hands of the living God" (Heb. 10:31).

In the Old Testament book of Leviticus, we are told a story of Nadab and Abihu, two of Aaron's sons, who:

"...took their censers, put fire in them and added incense; and they offered unauthorized fire before the Lord, contrary to his command. So fire came out from the presence of the Lord and consumed them and they died before the Lord. Moses then said to Aaron, "This is what the Lord spoke of when he said: 'Among those who approach me I will show myself holy; in the sight of all the people I will be honored."

Leviticus 10:1-3

In the New Testament book of Acts (Acts 5:1-11), after lying to the Holy Spirit and to the apostle Peter, God struck dead first Ananias, then Sapphira, and "Great fear seized the whole church and all who heard about these events" (Acts 5:11).

Should all these examples frighten us as we contemplate what God might do to us if we sin? Is God a terrifying being in front of whom we are to cower? No. The apostle John tells us, "There is no fear in love. But perfect love drives out fear, because fear has to do with punishment. The one who fears is not made perfect in love" (1 John 4:18). We need not "be afraid" of God but we *do* need to "fear" Him (honor, deeply respect, and hold Him in awe and reverence). The author of the book of Proverbs tells us, "The fear of the Lord is the beginning of knowledge, but fools [those who are morally deficient] despise wisdom and discipline" (Prov. 1:7). We are wise when we fear God, but if we listen, obey, and follow Him, we need never be afraid of Him.

GOD AS A BIRD

Due to a severe famine in Bethlehem, Elimelech and Naomi, along with their two sons, Mahlon and Kilion, immigrate to the land of Moab (read the Old Testament book of Ruth). Elimelech soon dies, but both Mahlon and Kilion settle down in Moab, marry Moabite women, and care for their mother, Naomi. About ten years later, both Mahlon and Kilion die, leaving their mother and their wives, Orpah and Ruth, destitute.

Naomi hears that the famine has ended so she makes preparations to travel back to Bethlehem. Orpah decides to stay in Moab with her own people but, despite Naomi's urging, Ruth insists on traveling to Bethlehem with Naomi to adopt her land, people, and God. They arrive in Bethlehem right at the time of the barley harvest, so Ruth, as allowed by law, gleans barley from the edges of the field and from that which the harvesters drop. Boaz, whose field she happens to choose, is impressed by her hard work and dedication and blesses Ruth,

> *I've been told all about what you have done for your mother-in-law since the death of your husband—how you left your father and mother and your homeland and came to live with a people you did not know before. May the Lord repay you for what you have done. May you be richly rewarded by the Lord, the God of Israel, under whose wings you have come to take refuge.*
>
> *Ruth 2:11-12*

Boaz eventually marries Ruth and also cares for Naomi. It is a wonderful story of sacrifice, loyalty, love, romance, and the evidence of the sovereignty of God.

Boaz uses the wings of a bird as a metaphor to describe the shelter, safety, protection, warmth, comfort, and care that Ruth would receive from the God of Israel. The psalmists also use this metaphor: "Keep me as the apple of your eye; hide me in the shadow of your wings" (Ps. 17:8). "How priceless is your unfailing love!

Both high and low among men find refuge in the shadow of your wings" (Ps. 36:7). "Have mercy on me, O God, have mercy on me, for in you my soul takes refuge. I will take refuge in the shadow of your wings until the disaster has passed" (Ps. 57:1). "He will cover you with his feathers, and under his wings you will find refuge; his faithfulness will be your shield and rampart" (Ps. 91:4).

Centuries later, Jesus also used this metaphor to describe Himself and His relationship with His people who have rejected Him. "O Jerusalem, Jerusalem, you who kill the prophets and stone those sent to you, how often I have longed to gather your children together, as a hen gathers her chicks under her wings, but you were not willing" (Matt. 23:37).

Jesus identifies the bird as a hen, and this is probably the bird referred to by Boaz and the psalmists. However, because ancient Palestine was a major flyway for a variety of migrating birds and was home to numerous species,[13] there may have been other birds observed that also used their wings to provide shelter for their young. The outer feathers of a hen's wings interlock and form a protective, water-resistant barrier, while the interior down feathers provide softness and warmth. Because the little chicks initially only have down feathers which are not water-resistant, they scurry under their mother's wings for safety during times of danger and inclement weather. This metaphor helps us see that God is also a place of safety to protect us during the storms in our lives.

God is also compared to an eagle, which is one of the most majestic birds mentioned in the Bible. These large birds were known for speed and strength, and God referred to Himself as a strong eagle with powerful wings when He described His choice of transportation to rescue His people from Egypt. "You yourselves have seen what I did to Egypt, and how I carried you on eagles' wings and brought you to myself" (Exod. 19:4).

Years later, as the Nation of Israel was about to enter the Promised Land, using the same metaphor, Moses sang a song to remind the people of what God had done for them. "In a desert land he found him, in a barren and howling waste. He shielded him and cared for him; he guarded him as the apple of his eye, like an eagle that stirs up its nest and hovers over its young, that spreads its wings to catch them and carries them on its pinions" (Deut. 32:10-11).

God is likened to a large majestic bird that is strong and swift but is also gentle and hovers over His young, shielding, caring, protecting, and guarding them because they are deeply treasured.

GOD AS A POTTER

A potter lived about a fifteen to twenty-minute walk outside the village of Huehuetenango, Guatemala, where I grew up in the 1950s as the son of missionaries. His throwing wheel was located on the front porch of his small house that stood only a few feet from the side of the country road. Since he was friendly and welcomed visitors who wandered off the road to witness his unique skill, our family would, on occasion, set aside a few hours to walk out to his house to watch him create clay pots, vases, dishes, and other common household items.

His potter's wheel consisted of two wooden discs attached to each other through their centers by a shaft of wood. The potter placed the clay on the upper, smaller, lighter disc, and as it spun in a counterclockwise direction, he deftly shaped it into his intended vessel. The upper disc spun as a result of turning the much larger and much heavier lower disc, and the momentum generated from spinning the heavy disc allowed the potter brief periodic pauses in the rhythmic forward and backward motion of his right leg as his bare foot smoothly pushed forward against the surface of the disc.

It always amazed me (and still does) how adept he was at perfectly centering the lump of clay on his disc, drawing it up into a cylinder, firmly and smoothly pressing the center of the cylinder downward, and then once again drawing it up into a hollow symmetrical object with walls of even thickness and curved contours. He made many different styles of clay articles. Some were for daily practical use such as carrying water from the stream or well or cooking tortillas or boiling soup, but others were ornamental and held no intended function other than adding beauty to someone's home. The potter spun his wheel and formed vessel after vessel according to his pleasure and his perception of the needs and desires of potential buyers. The clay was pliable and responded to each and every push and pull of the potter's hands.

Observing potters at work was most likely a common occurrence for those living in biblical times because vessels of pottery were routinely used. Therefore, when Job, Isaiah, Jeremiah, or the apostle Paul used the potter with his clay to describe the relationship of God with His people, they were probably able to easily relate to this perceptive metaphor.

In the midst of his intense suffering and sorrow, Job questioned God, "Your hands shaped me and made me. Will you now turn and destroy me?" (Job 10:8). Isaiah asked the people, "Does the clay say to the potter, 'What are you making?'" (Isa. 45:9b), and "You turn things upside down, as if the potter were thought to be like the clay! Shall what is formed say to him who formed it, 'He did not make me'? Can the pot say of the potter, 'He knows nothing?'" (Isa. 29:16). The apostle Paul expanded on this thought, "Shall what is formed say to him who formed it, 'Why did you make me like this?' Does not the potter have the right to make out of the same lump of clay some pottery for noble purposes and some for common use?" (Rom. 9:20-21). While speaking to God, Isaiah conceded, "Yet, O Lord, you are our Father. We are the clay, you are the potter; we are all the work of your hand" (Isa. 64:8). God, through Jeremiah, told the people, "Like clay in the hand of the potter, so are you in my hand, O house of Israel" (Jer. 18:6).

What does it mean that we are clay and God is our potter? This comparison is a small window into seeing and enriching our understanding of the sovereignty (one who possesses supreme authority[14]) of God. Most of us are fiercely independent. There is something inside us that rebels at the thought that God has all the "say" in who we are and what we do. Some living in the time of the apostle Paul questioned how God could create someone like Pharaoh (See Exod. 8-11) for the express purpose of showing His (God's) power to the world (Exod. 9:16), then punish him for his hard heart that refused to obey God. They could not see how this could possibly be an attribute of a caring and loving God.

Some of us may see the sovereignty of God as an interesting theological idea that is an intriguing topic for a friendly argument, but when it comes to living day after day and week after week, it is a frustrating concept and may lead us to think we have no control over our lives. This resignation could draw us to hopelessness, feelings of futility, frustration, annoyance, bitterness, or anger. We may ask, "What is the point of trying?" or, "Why bother?" We are, however, very responsible for our lives and how we live them. God's sovereignty and human responsibility are both true.

In gratitude, David tells God, "I praise you because I am fearfully and wonderfully made" (Ps. 139:14). God shapes, forms, and molds us according to His pleasure like potters mold their clay. God has fearfully and wonderfully made us—intricately and lovingly designed by the Master Creator—for a purpose, and our vocation is to live out that purpose as those who are created in the image of God (Gen. 1:27) and are to bear that image as lights in a dark world. "For we are God's workmanship, created in Christ

Jesus to do good works, which God prepared in advance for us to do" (Eph. 2:10).

"But God," I might lament, "I could fulfill your vocation for my life more competently if I wasn't so reserved or self-conscious. I would rather be outgoing and be able to stand up in front of a group of people and speak without fear. I would like to teach a Bible study class on Sunday morning without lying awake tense the night before. I could serve you so much more effectively if I didn't have chronic heartburn or nightly muscle pains that wake me up every night. If I wasn't so tired all the time, I could be more patient with others and have more energy to serve you. And ... a few extra IQ points would have been preferable, too. Why did you shape me the way I am?" We could undoubtedly all make our own list of self-viewed attributes that we would just as soon trade in for "better" ones. However, as our faith in our Potter grows, perhaps we can, in time, come to that place of thankfully resting and trusting in His sovereign purposes, love, and care.

EXPERIENCING THESE FACETS OF GOD'S CHARACTER

In August 1975, Cheryl and I loaded our meager belongings into an eight-foot U-Haul trailer, and towed it behind our 1972 Dodge Dart. We drove from Rochester, NY, to East Greenbush, NY, (a few miles southeast of Albany) so that I could attend Physician Assistant School for two years. I was to attend school full time and Cheryl was to financially support us by working as an activity director in a nursing home in Albany. I would need to get to school and Cheryl would need to get to work—each in a different direction—with only one car.

Needless to say, we were as "poor as church mice." In an attempt to live within our frugal budget, we carefully discussed every purchase to determine whether it was a "need" or a "want." When a repair was needed on the car, we deliberated the importance of the repair and carefully evaluated how long the car could safely run without the repair. I boldly ended the discussion with, "Well, we really need the car." Case closed! Find the money, pay for the repair, and keep our one car operating reliably. It was difficult with only one car but would have been impossible with no car. I had to get to classes and Cheryl had to get to work; it seemed like a rather logical and straight-forward decision.

We were renting a third of a house on a parcel of land that was situated on a country road. Although the road was not extremely busy, cars were not infrequent, and drivers, more often than not, sped over the hill just to the north of our house and down the slope past our driveway at inappropriate speeds. On one particular morning, one such driver flew over the hill and down the slope just as Cheryl was backing out of the driveway. Braking distance from the top of the hill to the driveway entrance was very short and he was unable to stop in time to avoid a "T-bone" collision with Cheryl and our 1972 Dodge Dart. It was a major blessing that, other than a few facial bruises, Cheryl, who was four months pregnant, was not injured.

The car, however, was very much injured. It was towed away by a small, local collision shop. The owner of the shop was unsure how long it would take him to repair the car, but he assured us he would work as quickly as possible. It turned out to be a full month before we reclaimed our car. His work was excellent, and the car looked better than it did before the accident, but ... a month?

Unfortunately, there was no money in our budget for a rental car, and our auto insurance policy did not include a rental car rider, so what were we to do? One of Cheryl's co-workers went out of her way to take Cheryl to work and bring her home each day. One of my classmates swung by and picked me up each day, then brought me back home again in the evening. Friends (whom we had only known for a few months) picked us up every Sunday and drove us back and forth to church services in Delmar, which was on the other side of the Hudson River. Friends, also on the other side of the river, drove over and back every week to take us to our Friday evening small group gathering.

It was incredible how people we barely knew were willing to go out of their way to help, love, and care for us during that difficult month. "Well, we really need the car." I guess not. God, using many different people, was able to provide for all our needs. I have never again taken our cars for granted. I am now certainly careful never to say, "Well, we really need _____."

God is a consuming fire and is jealous for our worship. We so easily "worship" other things by allowing them to be our source of security, meaning, or purpose. God wants to fulfill that role in our lives. Anything other than God that assumes that place in our lives is an idol. The apostle John thought this was so important that, in his first letter to a group of churches in Asia Minor (modern-day Turkey), he ended his letter with, "Dear children, keep yourselves from idols" (1 John 5:21). This is not as much about what we do, but the heart-level value we place on what we do. At the level of our deepest heart, what is the source of our security, meaning, and purpose? God is jealous for our worship because what we worship informs our motives, priorities, and decisions.

God, however, is not a scary, impersonal, cold deity who becomes angry when we don't worship Him. He is a parent who loves and cares for us and spreads His wings, so we have a place of refuge from the storms in our lives. He is a strong tower that protects us from the enemy of our souls. He is life-giving, thirst-quenching, clear, cold, living, spring water that refreshes us in the midst of our difficult situations. Because God shaped and formed us, He knows us better than we know ourselves, and we can trust that He has a plan to help us fulfill the purpose for which He created us.

What a rich storehouse of word pictures we've been given in the Bible to help enrich our understanding of God! There are many, many more than these five we've explored here. Study them and allow God to open your eyes to the amazing being that He is ... then bow and worship Him.

3

Enriching Our Understanding of the Church Through Metaphors

What thoughts come to mind and what emotions bubble up in your heart when you hear the word "church"? If you are, or have been, involved in a local church, has your personal experience predominately been positive or negative?

Philip Yancey, an internationally known Christian author and speaker, wrote a book entitled *Soul Survivor: How My Faith Survived the Church*.[1] In this book, he states that all authors have one major theme that tends to inform and guide their thoughts. "If I had to define my own theme," Yancey writes, "it would be that of a person who absorbed some of the worst the church has to offer, yet still landed in the loving arms of God."[2]

Commenting on a Facebook post, Dan Burruss remarked,

> *Susan, a self-professing Christian, began her Facebook comments with a curse on all pastors and churches. One of Susan's friends on Facebook asked her in response: "Do you hate churches and pastors?" Susan responded, "Yep." Her friend then asked a very insightful question: "Then I guess that means you hate Paul and Peter, and Jesus too." Susan proclaimed: "Oh no, not them, just*

all the ones around today." Then she added, "Jesus and I are doing great.[3]

Many people could recount their own stories of how the church disappointed them, hurt them, abused them, or exasperated them enough that they left the church altogether. Some of you were perhaps hurt by a pastor who treated you like a tool to advance their personal agenda, or you were hurt by a youth leader who sexually abused your teenage daughter, or someone in your small group slowly, over time, demeaned and humiliated you. Perhaps you were a pastor who finally resigned and quit the ministry because of those who degraded you, complained about everything you said or did, or consistently misunderstood and maligned your good intentions.

What are we to make of all of this? Is church a good thing or a bad thing? Does it add to our spiritual wholeness or detract from it? Is it a humanly contrived organization that is unnecessary but available for those of us who might choose to participate? If we prefer not to get involved in the church, can we say, "Jesus and I are doing great without it"? Since our decision to believe, receive, and follow Jesus is a personal one, why do we even need to get involved in a local church?

No matter what problems we may encounter in the church, we must understand that Jesus instituted it, loves it, died for it, and infuses it with power. While in Caesarea Philippi, Jesus asked His disciples what people were saying about who they thought He was. The disciples repeated some names they heard mentioned, like "John the Baptist," "Elijah," "Jeremiah," or "one of the prophets" (Matt. 16:13-14). Then Jesus asked them,

> *"But what about you?" ... "Who do you say I am?"*
> *Simon Peter answered, "You are the Christ, the Son of*
> *the living God." Jesus replied, "Blessed are you, Simon*

> *son of Jonah, for this was not revealed to you by man,*
> *but by my Father in Heaven. And I tell you that you*
> *are Peter, and on this rock I will build my church and*
> *the gates of Hades will not overcome it."*
>
> *Matthew 16:15-18*

Jesus says that the church He is building is so powerful "the gates of Hades will not overcome it" or "all the powers of hell will not conquer it" (NLT), or "not prevail against it" (ESV), or "not overpower it" (NASB). Because of Jesus' death on the cross, not only has the enslaving power of sin been broken, but this fledgling church will be so mighty it will vanquish the power of death and the power of Satan and his minions.[4]

The Greek word that is here translated as "gates" refers to immense doors found at the entrance to a prison, city, or very large building.[5] Jesus used this word picture to help us visualize the strength and invincibility of the church. This word picture brings to mind the gates of Mordor, as depicted in the movie "The Return of the King."[6] Near the end of the movie, in an attempt to distract Sauron's attention away from Frodo and Sam who are picking their way through the wastelands of Mordor to destroy the One Ring, the Army of the West led by Aragorn marches on Mordor. As Aragorn and his men approach the Black Gate, they appear puny and trivial in comparison to the dark, massive, impenetrable sixty-foot tall doors looming in front of them.

If we envision these enormous doors as a metaphor for the gates of Hades, we can begin to grasp a bit of a sense of the power of the church. Nothing can stand against it—not even the Black Gate of Mordor. If this is true—and it is—there can be nothing better than the church!

Where have we gone wrong? Why is the church so often known for its weaknesses rather than its strengths, its sickness rather than its health, and for the things it is against rather than the things it is for? Why is it known for hurting rather than healing, fatigue rather than refreshment, drudgery rather than delight, or routine rather than freshness?

First, we must remind ourselves that we have an unseen enemy who would like nothing better than to destroy the church. "Our struggle is not against flesh and blood, but against the rulers, against the authorities, against the powers of this dark world and against the spiritual forces of evil in the heavenly realms" (Eph. 6:12).

Second, Jesus chose to use humans to build His church, and we are imperfect people—always have been and always will be. We will always be prone to self-centeredness, pride, unforgiveness, and speaking ill of those who think differently than we do.

Third, our default is to focus on what we are to *do* in the church rather than who we are to *be*. We like measuring financial and numerical growth, prominence in our community, or prestige among the other churches in our area. It has been said that the ABC's of a healthy church are Attendance, Buildings, and Cash. In other words, a healthy church is one that is numerically growing, is involved in a building project, and collects substantial offerings each week.

We love drawing graphs (either literally or figuratively). Things we *do* can be plotted on a graph but *be* things cannot. If our focus is on numerical growth rather than heart growth, we are going to build a church where people feel like utensils and are encouraged to "wear themselves out for Jesus" or are treated like wallets that should regularly and more generously be opened.

Fourth, feeling significant or important is a universal human need. The church is an environment that is ripe for jockeying for prime leadership positions, strutting our gifts, and fanning our peacock feathers or, for pastors, to see the church as their kingdom where they can maintain control and "rule the roost."

If the church is to be the church that Jesus envisioned, our focus must be on who we are, not what we do, and on growing our hearts, not our attendance. Of course, we want to introduce many to Jesus' love. Of course, we want to worship, teach, learn, serve, feed the poor, and _____, but those *doing* things must sprout from *being* followers of Christ. If our main goal is to *do, do, do*, the purpose of our church will be reduced to keeping the gears of the church machinery functioning smoothly while our intimacy with Jesus slowly cools.

What is the church? Although mentally we may know the correct answer, our daily conversations betray us and reveal our subconscious definition that the church is a building. We tell each other things like: "Let's meet at the church before driving to the park," or "Please contribute to the fund-raising drive so we can repair the church roof," or "There will be a blood drive at the church this Tuesday." However, the Greek word that is translated into English as "church" is "ekklēsía" and means "the called out ones" and refers to a group of Christ-followers who assemble together, not to the building in which they gather.[7]

What does it mean to be "the called out ones" or the assembly of Christ followers? In many ways, the church is a mystery, so there is no easy answer to that question. As a result, biblical authors must resort to using metaphors[8] in an attempt to offer some clarity. Some of these metaphors equate the church to a field, a priesthood, salt, light, a temple, an army of soldiers, a team of athletes, a flock of sheep, a stone building, a household (family), a bride, a human body, and many more.

Perhaps one of the more well-known and used metaphors is the church as a family. Since God is our Father and we are His children, all of us in the church are brothers and sisters. Using this analogy, we try to orient our programming around getting to know each other, developing a closer emotional bond, helping each other, and being more involved in each other's lives. This is very good; but, if we are to understand and appreciate the full beauty, power, and significance of the church, we must explore, understand, and embrace all the metaphors. What does it mean for the church to be a body, a family, a team of athletes, an army of soldiers, a flock of sheep, a building composed of living stones, ... and the bride of Christ all at the same time? Do we live like a body this month, then a family next month, and so on? We can never truly understand it because it is a mystery. But, if we study, meditate, pray, and seek God's wisdom, the eyes of our hearts will begin to visualize the depth and richness of the church and, *as we see*, our churches will radically change.

Although for the purposes of this chapter, I will more thoroughly explore only the church as a body, I would encourage you to conduct your own study of the other metaphors. You will find a few Scripture passages noted below to get you started. Reflect, ponder, and meditate on each metaphor individually, but then bring them together into one integrated whole much like we do when we take a variety of musical instruments and bring them together into one orchestra. Each instrument with its unique key, pitch, tone, and volume range produces a pleasurable sound; but, when they are all played together in an orchestra and blend together as one, they create music that powerfully stirs our hearts. When we see, understand, and apply what we learn, our churches will flourish.

THE CHURCH AS A TEMPLE

While speaking about its dangers, the apostle Paul said, "Flee from sexual immorality ... Do you not know that your body is a temple of the Holy Spirit, who is in you, whom you have received from God? You are not your own; you were bought at a price. Therefore honor God with your body" (1 Cor. 6:18-20). We so often read verses like these and apply them individually to ourselves.

The church as a whole is also a temple, and anything I do to desecrate my body sickens the entire church. "Don't you know that you yourselves [plural] are God's temple [singular] and that God's Spirit lives in you? If anyone destroys God's temple, God will destroy him; for God's temple is sacred, and you ["you" is plural in the Greek] are that temple" (1 Cor. 3:16-17). God in all His glory, dwells in our church.

THE CHURCH AS AN ARMY OF SOLDIERS

The apostle Paul tells Timothy to "Endure hardship with us like a good soldier of Christ Jesus. No one serving as a soldier gets involved in civilian affairs—he wants to please his commanding officer" (2 Tim. 2:3-4).

THE CHURCH AS A TEAM OF ATHLETES

The apostle Paul frequently refers to the Christian life as an athletic competition. "Do you not know that in a race all the runners run, but only one gets the prize? Run in such a way as to get the prize" (1 Cor. 9:24). "Forgetting what is behind and straining toward what is ahead, I press on toward the goal to win the prize for which God has called me heavenward in Christ Jesus" (Phil. 3:13b-14). "If anyone competes as an athlete, he does not receive the victor's crown unless he competes according to the rules" (2 Tim. 2:5). "I have fought the good fight, I have finished the race, I have kept the faith" (2 Tim. 4:7).

THE CHURCH AS A FLOCK OF SHEEP

God is our shepherd and we are a flock of sheep. Shepherds were well known for how they cared for, fed, protected, and gave their lives for their sheep. Shepherds were very different from hired hands who would occasionally fill in for the shepherds. Hired hands weren't even responsible for the death of the sheep that were under their care. "If it was torn to pieces by a wild animal, he shall bring in the remains as evidence and he will not be required to pay for the torn animal" (Exod. 22:13). Shepherds, on the other hand, had a vested interest in the well-being of their sheep. Isaiah used the shepherd metaphor to emphasize that our mighty and powerful God is also tender and loving. "He tends his flock like a shepherd: He gathers the lambs in his arms and carries them close to his heart; he gently leads those that have young" (Isa. 40: 11). Jesus called Himself the Good Shepherd who gives His life for the sheep. He knows His sheep and His sheep know His voice (John 10).

The Church as a Stone Building

The apostle Peter said, "As you come to him, the living Stone—rejected by men but chosen by God and precious to him—you also, like living stones, are being built into a spiritual house to be a holy priesthood, offering spiritual sacrifices acceptable to God through Jesus Christ" (1 Pet. 2:4-5).

Each individual stone is strong and durable but, in itself, is of little value until it is mortared, or expertly cut, to closely fit to the stones around it. When all the stones join together, they form a strong building.

The Church as a Household (Family)

The apostle John excitedly proclaimed, "How great is the love the Father has lavished on us, that we should be called children of God!" (1 John 3:1). When we believe, receive, and choose to follow Jesus, we become God's children. God is our Father, and all of His children become spiritual brothers and sisters in God's household (family). The apostle Paul refers to us as "the family of believers" (Gal. 6:10), or "members of God's household" (Eph. 2:19); the apostle Peter refers to us as "the family of God" (1 Pet. 4:17).

THE CHURCH AS A BRIDE

The bride/bridegroom metaphor is powerfully portrayed throughout the entire Bible. The prophet Isaiah said, "As a bridegroom rejoices over his bride, so will your God rejoice over you" (Isa. 62:5b). God made a covenant with His chosen people and, throughout the Old Testament, referred to them as a prostitute when they worshiped and served other gods. The apostle Paul spoke of marriage as a shadow of our relationship with Christ. "For this reason a man will leave his father and mother and be united to his wife, and the two will become one flesh. This is a profound mystery—but I am talking about Christ and the church" (Eph. 5:31-32). The Book of Revelation reveals that "the wedding of the Lamb has come, and his bride has made herself ready" (Rev. 19:7b). This metaphor speaks of the "intimacy and mutual fidelity" that is not only expected between a husband and wife but also between the church and Christ.[9]

THE CHURCH AS A BODY

Augustine observed, "Men go abroad to wonder at the height of mountains, at the huge waves of the sea, at the long courses of the rivers, at the vast compass of the ocean, at the circular motion of the stars; and they pass by themselves without wondering."[10] An in-depth study of the human body never ceases to induce awe and wonder at its complexity, diversity, and interdependence. It is an amazing collection of organs that are each complete, separate, and independent, and yet, simultaneously, seamlessly, and inextricably connected and dependent on each other for survival.

The heart is self-contained and uniquely designed to receive blood from the body and pump it to the lungs, and to receive blood from the lungs and pump it back to the body. No other organ assists with this function; if the heart ceases to pump, the body dies.

The kidneys are encapsulated, distinct from the rest of the body, and exquisitely designed to maintain correct pH and filter impurities and excess salt from the blood. No other organ performs the kidneys' duties.

The lungs inhale oxygen-rich air and exhale carbon dioxide-rich air. No other organ helps with this crucial task.

Only the eyes can see, the ears hear, the nose smell, and the tongue taste. The intestines digest and absorb nutrients. The skin is a barrier to the outside world, keeping fluids in and microbes out. The thumb is uniquely designed for grasping and the big toe for balancing. The liver, gallbladder, and pancreas all have their distinctive responsibilities; and the appendix ... well, I'm not entirely sure what the appendix does, but I'm sure it is very important.

Although bones are hard, uncompromising, and inflexible, muscles would be useless without them. The brain, heart, and lungs would frequently be injured without the hard, boney protective shell of the skull and chest. In contrast to bone, skin is soft and richly supplied with nerve endings, making it very susceptible to bruises, abrasions, lacerations, and pain, but it also allows us to touch and feel our environment and to experience the warmth and pleasure of skin-to-skin contact with another human being. Bones and skin are very different from each other, but each fulfills a very unique and essential function that would not be achieved were they to become frustrated with their disadvantages and attempt to be more like the other.

Although each organ is designed for a distinct task that no other organ can perform, not one of them can survive without the others. Each organ is dependent on blood, which delivers nutrients and oxygen and removes harmful waste products. Blood, however, can only reach every cell in the body because of an incredible system of pipes that range in size from the largest arteries and veins to the tiniest, microscopic capillaries. Each organ is dependent upon electrical stimulation that is only possible because of a phenomenal network of miles of nerves that snake throughout the body. Guided by amazingly complex chemical feedback loops, hormones circulate throughout the blood turning organ functions on and off.

The human body is a spectacular display of independence and dependence, paradoxically, but seamlessly existing together without jealousy or power struggles.

This spring, as my wife and I shoveled, carted, and spread six cubic yards of mulch in four hours, I was very happy that my heart and lungs instantly and flawlessly responded and obeyed my muscles' instructions to provide them with additional oxygen and nutrients and to remove the increased accumulation of waste products. My heart and lungs never voiced a complaint that they had to work harder simply because the muscles demanded it. Instead, in full trust that a different part of the body was in need, they unhesitatingly responded accordingly.

I experienced the beauty of a smoothly functioning body as each organ, blood vessel, nerve ending, and hormone, specifically designed to perform a predetermined function, contributed to the mulch spreading cause. If one link, any link, had ceased to function as designed, the entire body would have suffered.

Although the apostle Paul likens the church to a body, this is not an original thought. Richard Hayes points out that in the ancient world, the body metaphor was commonly "used to urge members of the subordinate classes to stay in their places in the social order and not to upset the natural equilibrium of the body by rebelling against their superiors."[11] Paul, however, turns this metaphor upside down. He uses it, not to keep "subordinates" in their lowly status and "superiors" in their exalted status, but to place them all on equal footing, emphasizing equality, diversity, and interdependence. All are of equal value regardless of background: Jews, Greeks, slaves, or free (1 Cor.12:13).

Each of us in the church is an organ (member) in this body and therefore has a specific and crucial part to play if the church is to function smoothly and remain healthy. Paul said, "Just as each of us has one body with many members, and these members do not all have the same function, so in Christ, we who are many form one body, and each member belongs to all the others" (Rom. 12:4-5). Just as the head is the "control center" of our physical body, so also Christ is the "control center" of our spiritual body (the church) and therefore has authority over everything we do. "And he [Christ] is the head of the body, the church; he is the beginning and the first-born from among the dead, so that in everything he might have the supremacy" (Col. 1:18).

In his letter to the church in Ephesus, Paul used this metaphor to help us understand the nature and purpose of the church and how, when the church functions as a body, it can flourish.

> Now these are the gifts Christ gave to the church: the apostles, the prophets, the evangelists, and the pastors and teachers. Their responsibility is to equip God's people to do his work and build up the church, the body of Christ. This will continue until we all come to such unity in our faith and knowledge of God's Son that we will be mature in the Lord, measuring up to the full and complete standard of Christ. Then we

will no longer be immature like children. We won't be tossed and blown about by every wind of new teaching. We will not be influenced when people try to trick us with lies so clever they sound like the truth. Instead, we will speak the truth in love, growing in every way more and more like Christ, who is the head of his body, the church. He makes the whole body fit together perfectly. As each part does its own special work, it helps the other parts grow, so that the whole body is healthy and growing and full of love.

Ephesians 4:11-16 (NLT)

We need to be careful that we do not misinterpret Paul's opening comments. Some leaders believe it is their job (from somewhere "above" and "outside" the body) to train, teach, and direct the members to do the work of the ministry. These leaders teach while members work. However, when we compare this with Paul's thoughts in 1 Corinthians 12, it is clear that all Christ-followers are a part of the body—each with a unique, but necessary function. Although leaders are charged with the responsibility of training members, in some situations, leaders—also members of the body—must answer to non-leader members if a fully interdependent healthy body is to be maintained.

Leaders are not endowed with "a bit of each gift" so that they can tell everyone else how to do things. The leaders are not wiser and more knowledgeable than the rest of the body. Members are wisest in their area of gifting. Someone with the gift of hospitality is wiser in that area than a leader without that gift. For leaders to unilaterally make decisions concerning how guests are to be warmly welcomed and how welcoming environments are to be developed within the church's building and then instruct those with the gift of hospitality to implement those decisions is contrary to how a healthy body performs.

All Christ-followers have Holy Spirit-given gifts. They must willingly and naturally use them for the health of the overall body. If we do not use our gifts, we are like a non-functioning pancreas uselessly located in the abdominal cavity. Without a pancreas, not only would we be unable to digest the fats and proteins we eat because of a lack of digestive enzymes, but glucose would rise to toxic levels due to lack of insulin.

Just one organ neglecting to perform its function results in major disabilities that impact the health of the entire body. How many churches have to create music teams with willing people while gifted musicians sit unused in the pews? How many Sunday morning children's classes are taught by willing volunteers who view class time as "babysitting" while gifted teachers never volunteer? How many churches struggle to plan ahead, organize their ministries, and communicate effectively with the congregation while gifted administrators have no input?

Peterson equates this tragedy to living "stunted like acorns in a terrarium."[12] When acorns fulfill their God-given destiny, they grow to be sixty to one-hundred feet tall, add beauty, provide shade, release oxygen, supply shelter for birds, and contribute to our environment in many other ways. For this to occur, however, they must be planted in a wide-open space so that they might grow uninhibited—not confined to a six-inch-tall existence in a terrarium. I also love Benjamin Franklin's analogy. He quips, "Hide not your talents. They for use were made. What's a sundial in the shade?"[13]

Some members are happy to offer their gifts and talents, but only if they can function on their own with no input from others. That would be like the lungs saying they are happy to inhale oxygen and exhale carbon dioxide for the body, but then decide that breathing sixteen to twenty times a minute is perfectly adequate even when the body is rapidly running uphill. "I'd be happy to teach a children's class, but I don't like your curriculum, so I'll teach something different for my class." "I'd love to lead the music team, but we will need to change the type of songs we sing."

Some leaders want to make all the decisions but inevitably find they need help from others to accomplish their goals. Although they would never say it out loud, they would agree with Henry Ford when he lamented, "Why is it that I always get a whole person when what I really want is a pair of hands?"[14]

When part of the body suffers, the entire body suffers. Recently, one of my molars became so sensitive that even my tongue brushing against it caused severe pain. While waiting four days before my dentist could see me, despite pain medication, I couldn't eat, sleep, read, or settle into doing anything. My entire body was focused on surviving and getting just one minute closer to when the pain would end. It was amazing how one tiny collection of minerals, blood vessels, and nerves could bring my entire body to a halt. When the tooth was finally pulled, it was not just my mouth that rejoiced, but my entire body rejoiced. Paul says, "Rejoice with those who rejoice; mourn with those who mourn" (Rom. 12:15). This admonition is not yet another responsibility we dutifully have to add to our busy lives. It is not something we *do*; it is merely a description of who we *are*. If we are a body, that which impacts me impacts you, and what affects you affects me. The church body rejoiced with us when each of our boys was born, and it rejoiced with us—and helped us move— when we bought a house. It mourned with us when, at the age of twenty-nine, my brother died, and it mourned with us when, two months later, at the age of thirty-two, I was diagnosed with colon cancer. No matter what transpires in one portion of the body, the entire body experiences it and responds with rejoicing or grieving.

The church is a body, and with God's strength, we *can* live like one.

Experiencing the Church as a Body Through the Seasons of My Life

Childhood experiences.

My earliest church experiences occurred in a Spanish-speaking congregation in the town of Huehuetenango, Guatemala, where my parents were missionaries. At the time, I knew nothing about body metaphors, nor would I have been able to identify any of the attributes of a healthy church. All I knew was that I felt like I was an integral part of the church and felt loved, affirmed, connected, and warmly accepted. Why did I feel this way? What was it about the church that drew us all together as a body?

As I pause and allow my mind and heart to meander through my memories, I discover it was not the quality of the music team, the size of the church, the wisdom of my Sunday School teacher, the preaching ability of the pastor, or the creative variety of programs and activities. It was the consistent but ordinary and, perhaps to some, "insignificant" details and events that, for me, confirmed my place in the church body.

It was the friendly, warm, kind, and unhurried visits at people's homes. It was the fun times we had playing with friends in the church's large patio after the worship services. It was when a bunch of kids came over to our house to play soccer. It was when the entire church devoted a day to hike out to a park-like setting beside a river for a baptismal service followed by fellowship, games, and food. It was when a team of us traveled several miles to a nearby small village to offer Bible classes for children. These children were so poor that, when given a colorful picture cut from the front of a greeting card, they prominently displayed it on a wall, becoming a rare decorative piece of artwork in their home. During special occasions, it was the smell of the aromatic pine needles that were spread over the floor of the meeting room and the delicious tamale dinners that were served after the worship service.

It was when I grieved with one of my best friends, whose five-year-old sister had just died during open-heart surgery. It was when I helplessly and awkwardly stood there and witnessed the pain in his eyes and his anguish as they lowered her casket into the earth. It was the closeness I felt to him as I observed his suffering and, in my young mind, as best as I knew how, suffered with him.

It was the ministry trips with my friends and our pastor when we traveled out into the countryside for evangelistic meetings, and I went along to play my cornet as part of the musical "conjunto." Our band played for the time of singing, but we also provided special instrumental music during the service. I look back on those trips with fondness because not only were they filled with fun, but they were opportunities to bond with my friends and to minister to those living in poverty.

Each trip was an adventure and rarely routine. I remember one trip when, a few hours before the evening service, my friends and I ran down to the local river to swim. I hung my towel over a crude, makeshift split-rail fence, then jumped into the river. After a cool, refreshing swim, I wandered back to the fence to retrieve my towel, but it was nowhere to be found. As I stood there drip-drying and contemplating where it could have gone, out of the corner of my eye, I saw a cow chewing its cud with a bit more effort than usual. On closer inspection, I discovered a three-inch piece of white fabric hanging out of its mouth. I ran over and grabbed the short stub of terrycloth that still remained external to the cow's mouth and pulled as hard as I could.

After some effort, the cow finally relinquished its intended meal and out slid a tightly wound ball of green/yellow slime. As my friends laughed and commiserated with me, we ran back to the adobe hut to get ready for the evening worship service.

Although to some, this event hardly qualifies as an example of "church body life," it was a comical moment in my life—shared with my friends as we played and ministered together—that, unbeknownst to me at the time, was yet another incident that shaped my heart and instilled within me a love for the church.

Every five years, my parents returned to the United States for a year of furlough. One such furlough occurred when I was ten years old. Attending Sunday school classes with children I did not know was uncomfortable and far from a warm, fun, and caring place to be. It was especially difficult during the summer when our family spent three months driving thousands of miles visiting the churches that financially supported us. Every Sunday morning, I had to endure yet another new Sunday school class where the kids stared at me, wondering who I was and what I was doing in their class. By the end of that summer, I had developed a strong dislike for the church. It became clear to my young mind that church was a place for "regular kids," not for visitors.

Teenage experiences.

My school in Guatemala was composed of about forty missionary children, grades one through eight. After graduating, I studied alone using correspondence courses for ninth grade, then returned to the United States for tenth grade while my parents were again on furlough. We lived in Ventnor, NJ, and I attended Atlantic City High School, which was composed of not forty but two thousand students.

I remember it took me months to make the difficult transition from a tiny school in tranquil Huehuetenango to a large, difficult-to-navigate, four-floor city high school. We attended a large church not far from our apartment where I—a fifteen-year-old, wearing unmatching, out-of-style clothes, with an out-of-style haircut, and who didn't know how to relate to city or suburban

American teenagers—felt as awkward as I did at school. I was the tenth-grader to whom everyone was pleasant, but no one befriended. When I most needed to be a part of a church body, I was an outsider who didn't belong.

Young and middle-age adult experiences.

After I got married, my church experiences were varied. Due to moving and church hunting, we attended some six or seven churches for varying lengths of time until we settled into a small non-denominational community church where we remained involved for thirty-eight years. All of us in that church were imperfect people who, not infrequently, disagreed, became frustrated and annoyed with each other, and, on occasion, hurt each other. However, in the midst of it all, we grew in our relationships, laughed and cried together, and experienced what it means to be a body where we could use our gifts, serve, minister to each other, and reach out to those less fortunate than ourselves.

The four short-term mission trips in which we were involved were an illustration of the church at its finest. We were involved in each other's lives, took time to talk, worked alongside each other, ate meals together, and relaxed together in the evenings. We shared a common purpose, and all worked together to accomplish it.

There were two things I could never get used to. The first was the constant flow of people in and out of the church. In the thirty-eight years we were members, attendance varied from eighty to nearly two hundred, and literally, hundreds of people came, stayed a while, then left.

The second thing I never got used to was the generally accepted maxim that when we establish our time commitment priorities, it always should be God first, family second, and then church third. I've since discovered that that priority list is not unique to that church, nor is it only an idea from the past. When we moved in

2016, I quickly discovered that our current church also adheres to that same list of priorities, and journal articles continue to declare its legitimacy. Whoever came up with that list certainly did not find it in the Bible.

When we say "yes" to Jesus' gift of salvation, we become a part of the body of Christ. We then cannot say, "It is all about Jesus and me and, later, I'll see whether or not I get involved in a local church." As a Christ-follower, we belong to Christ's body—it's part of the deal. When we decide to believe, receive, and follow Jesus, God gifts us with the Holy Spirit, who lives in us, teaches us, counsels us, and imparts a spiritual gift to us that we are then to use in the church. Look through each one of the above-mentioned metaphors. They each apply to us immediately upon choosing to follow Jesus.

Even though this maxim establishes three separate boxes, there is no division between God, our earthly family, and our spiritual body—*none*. Our language, and our use of the priority list, betrays our inability to see this. According to this maxim, our relationship with God (which I assume is evidenced by things like reading our Bible and praying) takes priority over our relationship with our spouse and children (Does this mean, "God and me" doesn't intersect with "family and me"?). Our responsibility to our families (I suppose this involves things like going to work, keeping up the house, and spending time with them) takes priority over church activities (I suspect this includes things like teaching Sunday School, helping on the music team, or serving on the trustee board).

This list of priorities sends a clear message that the church must be kept in its place. The list tells us: "Don't misunderstand, the church is very good, but it has an agenda (that is distinct from God and family) that depletes our time and emotional energy that we must conserve for our families back home. God is up in heaven somewhere, my family is here, and the church is down the road. Each of the three, in their separate corners of the universe, needs our attention, but it is crucial that we keep our priorities straight so that, as we hop from box to box, we don't cheat any of them; but, if we do cheat one of them, be sure to cheat the church, not the family."

In reality, our church family, of which God is the Father, is our new family within which our earthly family functions—the three are inseparable. Instead of feeling the need to balance our priorities between these three boxes—that spiritually do not exist—the answer is to "fix" the church so that it becomes all that it was intended to be; not that to which it has become over the centuries. Is it fixable? If so, how do we do it? Can a church ever truly become a healthy and wholesome joyful family and flourishing body? My hope and prayer is that it can, but we need to throw out our old notions of how we *do* church and begin to understand God's desire for us to *be* the church. Carefully studying the biblical metaphors for the church will help us begin to see with the eyes of our hearts.

Post Retirement experiences

After loving and being loved and knowing and being known for thirty-eight years in one church, upon moving to a new community, the hunt for a new church was a struggle. I was suddenly a visitor again and sadly was no longer loved, known, or valued. As occurred in Ventnor so many years before, I was once again an outsider. Everyone was pleasant to me but no one befriended me. Happily, now, four years later, things are slowly beginning to change.

Even though my introverted nature makes the process more difficult for me, I need to continually remind myself that creating community requires reciprocal openness and humility. As Henri Nouwen encourages us, "Those who come together in mutual vulnerability are bound together by a new strength that makes them into one body."[15]

4

Grieving with Hope

Our lives are filled with adventure, routine, time alone, and interactions with others. We work and play, laugh and cry, enjoy each other and get angry at each other, eat, sleep, clean the house, and mow the lawn. But so much of what we do very quickly becomes a distant memory. Other events, however, remain etched in our minds and hearts. A brief encounter with someone fifty years ago leaves such an impression on us that even today we remember every minute detail. We still see their facial expression and hear their tone of voice. We still feel the sting of their reproof, distain, contempt, or shaming, or we still feel the warmth of their love, approval, acceptance, affirmation, or encouragement.

We remember some events because they were joyful milestones in our lives—our high school, college, or graduate school graduation, our wedding day, the birth of a child, or a major promotion at work. We remember other events because they redirected our lives in unexpected ways—a major move from one city to another, a loss of a job, or a cancer diagnosis.

Then there are those events that make such an impact on our minds and hearts that they stand alone and are so dramatic and life-altering that all other events in our lives revolve around them. As a result, we divide our lives into two parts. We catalog all other experiences as to whether they occurred "before" or "after" the life-altering event. While trying to recall when another event occurred, we might ask ourselves, "Now, what year did that happen? Let's see, was it before _____ happened, or was it after?" Our life-altering event may not have changed the course of history and the entire calendar system as when Jesus was born and all of history was divided between the years BC and AD, but our life-altering event was so dramatic that our *personal* calendar was forever divided between "before" and "after," and our life will now never be the same ... ever. A "new normal" has begun. In an instant, we walk across a line that now divides "before" from "after."

That life-altering experience occurred for me on November 14, 1992. In many ways, that day was no different from any other Saturday in November in Henrietta, NY. It was cold, and ominous snow clouds hung in the dark grey sky. Since it was a Saturday, I spent the bulk of the day doing home repair projects, but I am at a loss to remember exactly what projects were on my "to do" list for the day. Whatever I was doing, I stopped working in the late afternoon to allow time to clean up and get ready to drive with my wife, Cheryl, and our thirteen-year-old son, Nathan, to our church for a "pot-luck supper." Shortly after the meal began, our sixteen-year-old son, Ben, and two of his friends joined us. After eating and chatting with us for a while, they left. Later in the evening, Cheryl, Nathan, and I drove back home.

At 9:00 PM, Ben called to chat and ask permission to stay out late with his friends so they could see a movie. Little did I know that would be the last time I would ever talk with him. After an uneventful "rest of the evening," the three of us went to bed.

At 12:15 AM, the ringing of the telephone woke me from a sound sleep.

"Is this Mr. Stoddard?" the voice on the other end of the phone asked.

"Yes," I replied.

The woman continued, "Your son has been in a serious motor vehicle accident and is severely injured. He is here in the emergency room at Strong Memorial Hospital."

I found my strained, tense voice raising a few decibels as I asked, with more of a tone of a plea than a question, "Is he at least still alive?"

"Yes," she lied, "but we need you to drive down here as soon as possible."

Cheryl, who was lying beside me, now sat bolt upright and began to shake and panic. I held her a few seconds and then went into the next room to wake up Nathan and let him know what had happened. We all dressed quickly and drove the fifteen minutes to the hospital. It took all my willpower to stop and wait at each of the red traffic lights. My entire life had come to a standstill. In my present state of suspended reality, it felt odd and a bit curious that the rest of the world had not also come to a standstill. Didn't anyone know what had happened? Didn't anyone know I needed to get to the emergency room quickly? How could the traffic, although lighter than usual at 12:30 AM on a Saturday night/Sunday morning, still continue to lazily flow along oblivious to this catastrophic event in my life? A few people were walking unhurriedly along the sidewalks as though nothing had happened. Didn't anyone care? Everything had changed; nothing would ever be the same again. Didn't anyone else know that?

On entering the emergency room and identifying ourselves, we were directed to a small room where we waited for what seemed like an hour, but was, I'm sure, only a few minutes. The physician entered the room but never sat down. While standing, he said, "I'm sorry, we did everything we could." We asked if we could see Ben and he directed us to a gurney in an ER stall and then left. (Even after all these years, I still shake my head in amazement and disbelief at how untrained he was in dealing with grieving families.)

I lay my head on Ben's chest and was startled to discover that it was ice cold. For a second or two, that coldness felt odd until I reminded myself that Ben was no longer inside that body lying on the gurney. In my state of numbness and shock, all I remember feeling was a sense of loss. I do not remember being aware of any thoughts of disbelief, anger, or grief. I just felt a deep, deep sense of loss, not only for the loss of my son but also for the loss of a gigantic piece of my heart that died that night.

I have no idea how long I was there with that cold and lifeless body that used to contain my son—a happy teenager, full of life, and with a contagious smile. However long it was, it did not feel long enough. This was to be the last time I would ever hold him again. How was I, with my life at a complete standstill, to now live in a world that had not slowed down for one nanosecond? My brain felt as though I had just overdosed on antihistamines—still functional, still able to interact with others, but "foggy," "spacey," and "robotic." How was I to plan, orchestrate, and navigate my life on this new planet to which I had suddenly been transported against my will?

Still numb and in shock, we drove home where several friends from the church were waiting for us. In the living room, Cheryl began to recount some of her memories of Ben to those who had gathered around. I was soon overcome with grief and deep emotional distress, and I stood up, left the room, and walked into the den where I fell to my knees and began to sob uncontrollably.

Without truly understanding quite why or how, I began to worship God out loud. I praised Him and told Him how great He was and how much He was worthy to be praised. The words didn't feel like they were mine. I'm convinced they were words which flowed out of me from the Holy Spirit who wanted me, right from the starting blocks of this new journey, to see my grief through the big picture lens of God's greatness and love. I can now look back and see how that worship experience helped me gain perspective and gave me physical, emotional, and spiritual strength for the weeks and months ahead.

My life has not been, and will never be, the same. Frederick Buechner had it right when he quoted Mark Twain. "When somebody you love dies, Mark Twain said, it is like when your house burns down; it isn't for years that you realize the full extent of your loss."[1] That giant chunk of my heart that died that night never recovered. Over time, I learned to cope with it and live around it and despite it and, in a deeper way, I learned of God's unfailing love and faithfulness.

Whoever coined that often-quoted phrase "time heals all wounds" was wrong. Time does not heal, but time *does* lessen the *intensity* of the feelings of loss and grief. God heals our hearts—not by returning them to their original state before our catastrophic event and not by removing the grief and loss, but by helping us see the big picture of God's plan from eternity past, through the present, and into eternity future. He heals our hearts by giving us hope.

In his first letter to the church in Thessalonica, the apostle Paul said, "But we do not want you to be uninformed, brothers, about those who are asleep, that you may not grieve as others do who have no hope" (1 Thess. 4:13, ESV).

Ben is forever gone from this earthly life. I will never physically see or hold him again, but I have confidence that because of my belief (and because of Ben's belief) in the birth, life, death, burial, and resurrection of Jesus, I will see Ben again and, when I see him again, it will be for eternity. This gives me hope for the future, but is this all there is to "hope"? Hope that one day I will see Ben once again? It is great that I will see Ben again, but I want to see him *now*! I miss him *now*! What does it really mean to "grieve with hope," and does it make any difference in my journey of grief?

Nicolas Wolterstorff, who lost his twenty-five-year-old son Eric to a mountain climbing accident, described his experience of "grieving with hope" like this:

> *Elements of the gospel which I had always thought would console did not. They did something else, something important, but not that. It did not console me to be reminded of the hope of resurrection. If I had forgotten that hope, then it would indeed have brought light into my life to be reminded of it. But I did not think of death as a bottomless pit. I did not grieve as one who has no hope. Yet Eric is gone; here and now he is gone; I cannot talk with him, now I cannot see him, now I cannot hug him, now I cannot hear of his plans for the future. That is my sorrow. A friend said, 'remember, he's in good hands.' I was deeply moved. But that reality does not put Eric back in my hands now. That's my grief. For that grief, what consolation can there be other than having him back?*[2]

I can certainly identify with Wolterstorff. My brain also mentally knows all the right answers. I know all about how hope should inform my grieving. My brain also does not need to be mentally reminded of the hope we have in the coming resurrection and the time when we will be reunited with our loved ones. But is that all "hope" boils down to—"being reunited with our loved ones"? Does the hope we are promised when we believe in the birth, life, death, burial, and resurrection of Jesus and accept His gift of salvation only refer to when we "go to heaven when we die"?

Please do not misunderstand. That is a huge part of our hope and a *very important* part of our hope. My hope of seeing Ben again once I get to heaven is wonderful and gives me strength for my journey of grief. But is that all? Are we left without consolation or comfort right now? Hope for the future is reassuring, but what about hope for right now—right now in the midst of my grief, pain, and suffering?

What does it mean to grieve *with hope*? What *is* hope? In using the word "hope" in our twenty-first century American culture, we might say things like:

- "I hope I pass my exam."
- "I'm getting married today so I hope it doesn't rain."
- "I hope I find a place to park downtown for the concert."
- "I hope my grandson wins the Pinewood Derby race."
- "I hope this new tree I'm planting doesn't die."
- "I hope my cancer doesn't return."

We hope for results that may or may not occur. We are uncertain about the outcome, but we "hope against hope" they will end in the way we wish them to end. This hope is wishful thinking. This hope is a wish we desperately want to come true but are not certain, nor will we ever be certain, if it will come true. But this twenty-first century American culture usage of the word "hope" does not give us the true meaning of the word as the apostle Paul used it or as other biblical authors used it.

Biblical hope has a much different meaning. When biblical authors use the word "hope" it means we can have a "confident expectation" or "solid assurance" that what we hope for will occur.[3] Biblical hope is the "desire of some good *with the expectation of obtaining it*"[4] (emphasis mine).

How can the apostle Paul have a confident expectation and solid assurance he will obtain that for which he hopes? How can he so positively encourage other followers of Jesus to have the same confident hope? Is the *object* of their hope only to once again see their departed loved ones in heaven? Clearly, if we believe in the death and resurrection of Jesus and accept His gift of salvation, we can grieve with the full expectation or assurance of seeing our departed loved ones again, but is that all? Is that the *object* of our hope? Because Jesus lived, died, and conquered death, those who believe in Him will also rise to meet those who preceded us in death, and we will live with them for eternity. This is great news; this is marvelous news! It gives us a solid assurance that we will be reunited with those we love. But is that where hope ends? It certainly and absolutely includes this, but there is *much more.*

The *object* of our hope is not that we might once again see our departed loved ones. The *object* of our hope is God, His unfailing love, and His promises. We cannot solidly believe His promises concerning our life after death while clinging to "wishful thinking" related to His promises for today. Our hope is in God. Our confident expectation and solid assurance are in God—who He is, His character, His Name. Who He *is* never changes. Who He *is* spans from eternity past to eternity future. Our few years here on earth are included in that eternal time frame or, rather, as God would view it, eternal "timeless" frame. Our hope in God spans the ages. When we "grieve with hope," we place our hope in a God who will not only reunite us with our loved ones someday, but who also will closely walk with us in the midst of our grief.

God is delighted when we place our hope in Him. The psalmist said, "The LORD delights in those who fear him, who put their hope in his unfailing love" (Ps. 147:11), or "The LORD takes pleasure in those who fear him, in those who hope in his steadfast love" (ESV). In the Hebrew language, the word "delights" or "takes pleasure" was often used to refer to God's delight or deep pleasure in the sacrifices that were offered to Him by worshippers who loved Him and obeyed Him.[5] It brings God great delight, satisfaction, and pleasure when we fear Him. Fearing Him does not mean we are afraid of Him, but that we hold Him in awe and reverence and are careful to do what He asks of us. The Scriptures are abundantly clear that God loves it when we fear Him, reverence Him, and obey Him.

However, right in the same sentence, right in the same breath, the psalmist states that God takes just as much delight in us when we place our hope in His unfailing love, or His steadfast love. The Hebrew word used here that is translated as "unfailing love" or "steadfast love" is "hesed love." It is "one of the richest and most theologically insightful terms in the OT. It denotes kindness, love, loyalty, and mercy."[6] This incredible love forms the foundation of His character and how He treats us: it is the foundation for His goodness, kindness, and faithfulness.[7] As the psalmist says, "The LORD is compassionate and merciful, slow to get angry and filled with unfailing love" (Ps. 103:8, NLT).

In the midst of my grief, it is difficult to place my hope in God, to place my assurance and confident expectation in His loyal love, His goodness, His faithfulness, His kindness, and His great compassion. In the midst of my grief, it can be disorientating to affirm that these words actually define the love of a God that "allowed my son to die."

It's not simple to grieve with hope. To grieve with hope is to know, deep within our hearts, that no matter how we feel, God's love is unfailing, merciful, and loyal. Tough stuff. Placing our hope in a God we feel has let us down is complicated. Our frail brains and feeble dehydrated hearts struggle to understand it. That is why God delights in us when we truly place our hope in His unfailing love. He knows this is not easy for us. When we hope in the midst of our confusion, we rest in the arms of a loving God who is full of goodness, mercy, grace, and kindness.

We must acknowledge there is much of God we will never understand. It is a mystery to us, but it is never a mystery to God. Job had to come to that place where he paused, remained silent, and allowed God to bring some perspective to his catastrophic situation (see Job 38-41). I, like Job, need to pause, remain silent, and allow God to speak deeply into my soul.

I do not need to understand everything about God to place my hope in Him and rest in His unfailing love and goodness.

If we truly *know*, not just in our brains but in the deepest recesses of our hearts, that God's very nature and character is love and we place our hope in Him, will it change the character and direction of our grief? I suspect so. Even twenty-eight years after Ben's death, I'm still trying to wrap my brain and heart around all of this. In the midst of my grief, it is very easy to lose heart, but the psalmist encourages us, "Be strong and take heart, all you who hope in the LORD" (Ps. 31:24). We can take heart because our hope is in God and in His unfailing love and promises, not just in the "resurrection of the dead." Our hope is in His character and goodness and in the unfailing love He pours over us every minute of our lives in the midst of our doubt, anger, disappointment, depression ... or whatever else we are dealing with. God loves us and is with us every minute of every day. We can't understand it all, but when we place our hope in God, we can live in the mystery of who He is and in His plan for all of eternity.

The psalmist talks to his own inner being and encourages himself to keep on keeping on in the midst of tough times. He says, "Why are you cast down, O my soul, and why are you in turmoil within me? Hope in God; for I shall again praise him, my salvation and my God" (Ps. 42:11, ESV).

When we turn our hearts and minds to hope, we can praise God and once again remind ourselves of the truth of who He is, what He has done in the past, what He is doing now, and the promises of what He will do in the future. As Buechner says, "Hope stands up to its knees in the past and keeps its eyes on the future."[8]

We cannot live in the present without remembering and reminding ourselves of what God has done in the past and placing our hope in what He will do in the future. We can love God and place our hope in Him only because He first loved us and gave Himself for us. "This is real love—not that we loved God, but that He loved us and sent His Son as a sacrifice to take away our sins" (1 John 4:10, NLT).

We need to pause and remind ourselves of the depth of this love. "For God loved the world so much that he gave his one and only Son, so that everyone who believes in him will not perish but have eternal life" (John 3:16, NLT). Jesus came and lived among us. He endured rejection from those whom, in love, He created and, at the end of His life, He endured torture with horrific scourging and death by crucifixion. Who would ever endure something like that for the love of another? Jesus did. Why? Because that is how much He loves us. Jesus knows our grief, our suffering, and our struggle. He knows we struggle in the midst of our grief to return His love and place our hope in Him. Buechner says it this way,

> *The words 'You shall love the Lord your God' become in the end, less a command than a promise. And the promise is that, yes, on the weary feet of faith and fragile wings of hope, we will come to love him at last as from the first he has loved us—loved us even in the wilderness, especially in the wilderness, because he has been in the wilderness with us. He has been in the wilderness for us. He has been acquainted with our grief.*[9]

How does all this change our grieving? Are we to stop grieving, keep a stiff upper lip, smile broadly, and pretend everything is fine? Because, after all, God is good and He loves us and will walk with us and we'll see our loved one again when we get to heaven.

The apostle Paul does not say we are not to grieve, but we are not to grieve *as those who have no hope.* Jesus grieved. Jesus cried at the tomb of Lazarus. He loved Mary and Martha and grieved right along with them even though He knew in a few minutes He would bring Lazarus back to life.

Death was never meant to be, but the penalty of sin is death, and we have grieved death ever since Adam and Eve ate the forbidden fruit in the Garden of Eden. Jesus loves us and knows what we are going through and never expects us not to grieve death. So what does hope in God mean in the midst of our grief? Death is not a period at the end of the sentence describing our life; it is only a semi-colon because our lives here on earth are only a nanosecond in comparison to all of eternity. It matters not if we live a few hours, a few days, sixteen years, thirty years, or ninety-five years. It is all less than a fraction of a blink of an eye in comparison to living forever after our earthly lives come to an end.

And from eternity past to eternity future, God loves us with a love our human brains cannot conceive. Being able to see this big picture removes a bit of the intensity of the grief. It removes some of the "sting" of the grief. In his first letter to the church in Corinth, the apostle Paul quoting from the Old Testament books of Isaiah and Hosea said, "Death has been swallowed up in victory. Where, O death, is your victory? Where, O death, is your sting?" (1 Cor. 15:54b-55). Because we place our hope in God, although we still weep, our tears need not be quite as bitter. Our loss is not irretrievable; someday we will be reunited with our loved ones. Although our grief is very real, it is not as gut-wrenching as it might be if we had no hope of ever seeing them again.

Our hope also leads us to a confident expectation and solid assurance that we will experience God's unfailing love, compassion, goodness, kindness, and faithfulness each day of our lives. Even while we walk "through the valley of the shadow of death," (Ps. 23:4) we need not fear because God is with us. We would all much more prefer to not walk in the valley, but life does not always grant us prolonged periods of hiking on the mountain tops. We will walk in the valleys at times; but, because of our hope in God and His unfailing love, we can be assured that we will never walk alone.

Because of our hope, during the "winter" of our lives, we can be assured that God will cause flowers to grow beneath the heavy snow of our grief. As the snow begins to melt in the garden outside our home in March, it is amazing to find beautiful hellebore flowers already fully developed and growing beneath the snow.

How did these flowers develop beneath the weight and freezing cold of winter snow? To me, it seems impossible! But there they are at the end of each winter, evidence of the hand of God lovingly creating beauty beneath the surface in the midst of the apparent absence of life. I saw these "winter flowers" poking up in the icy winter cold of my life through the voice of one of Ben's friends who shared how much Ben had meant to him. I saw them in the voice of one of my friends who told me Ben's funeral had revived her struggling faith, and in the letter of an inmate in Virginia who somehow had heard of Ben's life and death and had committed to follow Jesus (I still don't know exactly how all that transpired). I saw the promise of winter flowers in notes left at the gravesite, and in the slow but steady appearance of evidences of the thawing and rehydrating of my heart. These and many more examples are beautiful hellebore flowers created by the hands of a loving, compassionate God and growing beneath the cold, heavy snow of my winter.

Grieving with hope is easy to discuss but not easy to live. I've discovered my brain knows much more than my heart. It is easy to know all the right answers and have my theology all arranged and filed in neat categories, but it is very difficult to allow all that theology to reach my heart and inform my journey of grief. God, however, is loving, gentle, patient, and kind. In my life, I've discovered that knowledge seeps down from my head to my heart when I soak in God's presence every day and allow Him to pour His living water into my dehydrated heart. Spending quiet time in God's presence (See Chapter 6: "Spending Time Alone with God") has helped me begin to see more clearly—with my heart, not just my brain—how great a God He is, and it has helped my heart open its hands to appreciate and live in the mystery of all that I, as a human, will never understand. And, yes, someday, I *will* see Ben again as he runs to me with open arms and a big smile on his face.

5

Trusting God

Whether we read it online or in the newspaper or we hear it on the radio or watch it on the television, the daily news is never complete without a story on those who are suffering the consequences of a tragic event in their lives.

We hear of a loved one killed in a motor vehicle accident or shot by police. We hear of those who were sexually abused by a trusted authority figure, friend, or family member. We hear of global catastrophic events such as tornadoes that rip through neighborhoods killing people and destroying property. We hear of category-4 hurricanes that destroy homes and knock out the power grid to an entire island or cause severe flooding of coastal communities and cities. Terrorist attacks kill hundreds or thousands. There are mass shootings at concerts, night clubs, elementary schools, and churches. We hear of children killed from chlorine gas attacks.

To all these daily reports we can add our own personal stories of pain, suffering, and grief. To those not close to us, our stories may not seem as dramatic. Perhaps our pain and suffering stems from generational poverty, or living in a marriage struggling to survive, or living year after year unsuccessfully trying to become pregnant, or fighting a long battle with cancer. Or maybe we've been fired and can't find a new job, or _____.

In the midst of all this, we voice, or hear others voice, questions concerning God such as: "Where is God in all of this?" "Is God sovereign (possessing supreme authority[1])?" "If so, did these events slip by Him?" "Was He busy when He turned around and said, 'Oops'?" "Is God good?" "Can a God who is good allow such suffering?" "Is God Almighty, or all-powerful?" "If so, could He have prevented all of this from happening?" "If so, why didn't He?" "If He could but didn't, is He truly good?"

For most of us, our heads would say, "Yes, of course, He possesses supreme authority, is good, and is all-powerful," but our hearts aren't always quite so sure. We can more easily affirm God's sovereignty, goodness, and power when the pain and suffering occurs "out there" somewhere, to someone we don't know; but, when it happens to us personally or to a close family member, our hearts struggle a bit—or a lot.

In the early 1930s during the Great Depression, James Braddock brought hope to millions when, out of obscurity and poverty, he became the heavyweight boxing champion of the world.

Cliff Hollingsworth's 2005 movie "Cinderella Man," directed by Ron Howard and starring Russell Crowe and Renée Zellweger, dramatized this portion of Braddock's life. Before his success, his life was bleak. Despite the winter cold, his electricity and heat were turned off because he could not pay his bills. His family had very little food so, because they could not feed their children, his wife Mae sent them to live with relatives. Work became scarcer. He couldn't even earn a few dollars in minor boxing bouts because his right hand was broken in three places.

There is a scene in the movie when Jim and Mae sit down at the table for a meager dinner together. She reaches for his hands to hold them during their usual pre-meal prayer of blessing and thanksgiving; but, with a mixture of dejection, discouragement, disappointment, and resignation, he gently but firmly pulls his hands away from hers and says, "I'm afraid I'm all prayed out."

Isn't that how we sometimes feel? "No point in praying anymore; God isn't going to answer and help me anyway." We're unlikely to say this out loud, or even admit to ourselves that's how we feel. After all, since we know how we're *supposed* to think, our minds quickly suppress and bury our heart's pain somewhere "out of sight and out of mind." We quickly rebuke ourselves and say, "Of course, God is sovereign, good, and almighty. Of course, He will hear my prayers and help me. Of course, He loves me." We push our feelings of doubt and discouragement aside and keep on keeping on—frequently with a smile on our faces.

But what happens to our relationship with God when we put on a happy face and trudge through life, ignoring the condition of our hearts? We develop a subtle, oftentimes subconscious, frustration or disappointment with God. Or we resign ourselves to, "That's just the way it is. I don't understand it, but I'm sure God does." Or we may think, "Doesn't God want me to be happy? I certainly know what would make me happy... doesn't He? Actually, I've told God multiple times how He can make me happy; why doesn't He just do it? Since I know what would bring me meaning, joy, peace, and contentment, if He loved me, wouldn't He want the same things for me? I mean, God doesn't even need to figure it out; if He would just do what I asked Him to do, everything would be fine." Or, perhaps more to the point, "If He *really* loved me, He wouldn't have let _____ happen in the first place."

What is the result of this line of thinking? Deep inside, sometimes without even being aware of it, we begin to believe God cannot be trusted—not really—maybe in a vague global way, but certainly not in *my* daily life. We certainly would never say this out loud; after all, our brains clearly know we are *supposed* to trust God.

What does "trusting God" really mean? How does it actually look as we each live our daily life? What is the *object* of our trust? That God will keep us "safe" from injury, illness, or problems? That God will keep us happy? That God will keep our life running smoothly? That God will "fix" things for us? Or, is our trust to be in God who created us, sees us, knows us, loves us, and knows what is best for us? Our trust is to be in a sovereign, good, almighty God, even when we don't understand what's happening to us in the midst of life's storms. It may be easy to verbalize and give mental assent to all this, but our hearts sometimes have a difficult time embracing it.

What does the Bible have to say about trusting God? The author of the book of Proverbs said, "Trust in the LORD with all your heart, and do not lean on your own understanding. In all your ways acknowledge him, and he will make straight your paths" (Prov. 3:5-6, ESV). Trusting is a "recognition of who God is and who we are."[2] Trusting means we "depend on [someone] with the sense of being completely confident and feeling utterly safe."[3] Trusting in God means we move quickly to refuge.[4]

When we know who God is and feel utterly safe and confident in His care, we can run quickly to find refuge in Him. Imagine we are mountain climbing. As we near the summit, an unexpected storm blows in with a heavy, drenching rain. Loud claps of thunder and dramatic bolts of lightning crisscross the sky. Our first thought might be, "We're dead up here on this mountain!" But just then, we spy a cave along the side of the trail not far away and, placing our trust in the cave, we run into it for safety. We trust that it will protect us from the storm. We are now in the cave, safe from the raging storm outside. That is the picture of what happens when we trust in God. Yes, I know it's easy to "see" what it means to trust in a physical cave to protect us from a physical storm, but what does it mean to trust God in this same way in the midst of the "storms" in our lives? Do we feel utterly safe and confident in His care in the midst of the storm? Do we move quickly *to Him* for refuge? It is mentally easy to affirm that God is my refuge and place of safety in the midst of the storms in my life; but, when the storms come, does this mental knowledge give me peace? Do I feel protected? Not usually! Usually, no matter how much I pray and say I place my trust in God, I still feel like I am unprotected out in the midst of the drenching rain, claps of thunder, and bolts of lightning that are all around me. Why doesn't "knowing the right stuff" help me?

The passage in Proverbs states I am to trust God's wisdom and knowledge, not my own, but what does that mean? God gave us brains and He expects us to use them, right? How do I know if I'm leaning on God's wisdom or on my own? These verses also contain a promise. If I trust God as I should, God will make my paths straight; He will straighten out the crooked road and make it even and smooth. Wow, that sounds great! That is what I want! But, how do I really do it? How do I truly trust God with all my heart? How do I truly experience Him as my shelter during the storms of my life? Is it even possible and, if so, how?

The prophet Isaiah wrote, "You will keep in perfect peace those whose minds are steadfast, because they trust in you. Trust in the LORD forever, for the LORD, the LORD himself, is the Rock eternal" (Isa. 26:3-4). These verses start right off with a promise. If we trust in God, our minds will be steadfast, and He will keep us in perfect peace. That is exactly what I want and need! I would love for my heart to be at peace! When I truly trust in God, my mind is "steadfast." Other translations use the word "fixed" or "stayed." The Hebrew word translated as "steadfast" means our hearts are firmly supported and sustained[5] as we lean upon, or brace ourselves,[6] against something. In this case, we are to firmly lean upon, brace, and support ourselves against God, *the* Rock.

Picture one of those mammoth rocks on the shore of the ocean, totally unmovable despite the huge waves crashing on it day after day and year after year. We would never rely on our own strength to keep from being washed out to sea or thrown into shore by the unrelenting waves; we would lean on, and brace ourselves against, the rock. We trust the rock to keep us steadfast, immovable, firmly supported, and sustained. It's easy to see how we can depend on a physical rock to support us and protect us from the crashing waves, but how does this all work with THE Rock? How can we have a steadfast mind and brace ourselves against God? It is a lot more difficult to conceptualize this in the spiritual realm. I can't see God or feel Him or wrap my arms around Him. When I try to be steadfast in the storms of life, it doesn't always seem to "work" for me. Even though I believe all the right things and say all the right things and pray really hard, I'm still just as anxious and unable to truly trust God to sustain me in the crashing waves of my life. Is it even possible to truly trust and remain at peace?

The psalmist invites us to "Taste and see that the LORD is good: blessed is the one who takes refuge in him" (Ps. 34:8).

When my grandson was younger, he frequently was reluctant to try any new foods. If it didn't look familiar, he refused to try it. I found myself frequently encouraging him to "Just taste it." I asked him, "How can you know whether or not you'll like it if you don't taste it?" The psalmist may be thinking, "Don't say God can't be trusted or doesn't love you. How do you know if you don't *taste* Him? You need to taste and see!" We need to experience God for ourselves. The psalmist is saying, *Check Him out! Try Him!*

Each of us needs to taste and see for ourselves what it means to take refuge in God. When we do, we'll see that God is very good. The Hebrew word for "take refuge" is very similar to the word "trust," but it is even more urgent. Trust means to move quickly to refuge. Take refuge means to *flee* for protection.[7] So if we are on a mountain climb and it begins to pour rain, and the thunder is deafening, and the lightning bolts are flashing one right after the other, and suddenly a bolt of lightning splits a tree straight down the middle just ten feet away from us, we will *flee* to the cave.

Again, it is easy to see how this all plays out in our physical lives as we imagine a severe storm while on a mountain climb, but how does it "work" in our spiritual/emotional lives? It is not easy! It's not easy to trust God whom we cannot see or touch, or whom we think has let us down and we are beginning to doubt His love for us. At least it has not been easy for me.

My Journey of Trust

My journey of trust began long before I placed my personal faith in Jesus as my Savior. As it does with all of us, it began many years before I was born. Both sets of my grandparents were missionaries in Africa. They devoted their lives to serving God on a continent on the other side of the Atlantic by taking the good news of God's love to those who had not yet heard it. Both my parents grew up in Africa and were shaped by the faith and trust of their parents. Upon marrying, they chose to devote their lives to serving God in the Central American nation of Guatemala. Before I was born, while my parents were still in Columbia, South Carolina, God knew me and formed me. As the psalmist said:

> *For you created my inmost being; you knit me together in my mother's womb. I praise you because I am fearfully and wonderfully made; your works are wonderful, I know that full well. My frame was not hidden from you when I was made in the secret place. When I was woven together in the depths of the earth, your eyes saw my unformed body. All the days*

*ordained for me were written in your book before one
of them came to be.*

Psalm 139:13-16

At the age of two, I sailed with my parents on a banana boat from Miami to Costa Rica, where my parents attended language school for two years before traveling north to Guatemala. I then lived in Guatemala from four to sixteen years of age. I placed my faith in Jesus as my Savior sometime before the age of twelve. I "said the words" to ask Jesus to come into my heart many times over those first years of my life. I was never sure if I'd really said it, or said it right, so I kept repeating it "just in case."

Finally, sometime between the ages of ten and twelve, I clearly remember telling Jesus that if I hadn't done it before, I really was doing it this time. From that moment on, I never again doubted my place in God's family and, at the age of twelve, I was baptized in a river out in the countryside near a small town in Guatemala. Later, at the age of sixteen, while at a Christian summer camp, I recommitted my life to Jesus and made it clear that I would truly follow and obey Him.

Knowing that during my teen years I would have to leave my home in Guatemala to attend high school in the United States, I was trained to be self-reliant and independent. I grew up learning how to be in control and on my own. These are good qualities, right? Well, as it is with most things, there are usually two sides to who we are and who we are becoming. Over time, I became confident and felt I knew the best way to do most anything. Although I knew I needed other people to help me, and I certainly readily accepted help for my physical needs, unbeknownst to me at the time, emotionally, I had become self-sufficient, independent, pompous, and arrogant. Without realizing it, I had slowly built a wall around my heart and emotionally closed everyone out of my life. Unfortunately,

I was totally unaware that at an emotional/heart level, I didn't think I needed God either. I certainly trusted Him and depended on Him and followed Him with my brain but not at the level of my heart. When things, in general, were going well, I was unaware of that brain/heart discrepancy. When problems occurred, I prayed and trusted that God would fix them and, for the most part, He did. I served Him and obeyed Him and expected that in return, He would bless me, keep me safe and healthy, and keep my life flowing smoothly. That arrangement and approach to "trusting God" seemed to work pretty well for the first thirty-two years of my life.

At the age of thirty-two, my nearly thirty-year-old disabled brother unexpectedly died in his sleep. Two months later, I was diagnosed with colon cancer. These were the first "major" problems in my life.

"What's going on? Those are the things that happen to other people, aren't they? They shouldn't happen to me. After all, if I pray and trust God, He will protect me and 'bad things' won't happen to me, right?" My unspoken but assumed bargain with God had worked pretty well up until then. What happened? I was still obeying and serving God, and I trusted that God would keep His side of the contract and continue to bless me, keep me safe and healthy, and keep my life flowing smoothly.

I grieved the loss of my brother, endured the painful radiation treatments for my cancer, and prayed a lot. Back then, there was a high recurrence rate for that type of cancer, so many were praying, and I trusted God to heal me. I endured frequent follow-up visits and waited. After seven years, I began to breathe easier knowing that, at that point, the cancer probably wouldn't recur. I "trusted" God and He came through for me and removed the cancer, once again confirming for me that He was keeping His end of the bargain and that, yes, indeed, "God was sovereign, God was good, and God was

Almighty." Right? Isn't that what trusting God is all about? Isn't our trust to be in a God who will keep all our stuff fixed?

When I was forty-two years old, our older son, at age sixteen, was killed in a motor vehicle accident. I grieved and accepted the tragedy as a part of life. I've since learned that *acceptance* is not the same thing as *trust*. One month later, I began to get frequent heartburn which, over the months that followed, continued to get worse and worse despite very heavy doses of medication. Finally, four years later, I had surgery to create a functional valve above my stomach to keep the stomach acid where it belonged. That made a significant difference, but the heartburn persisted at a lower intensity.

A year later, although I thought it wouldn't make any difference, I went to a chiropractor for my heartburn problem. The chiropractor discovered very tight upper back muscles of which I was totally unaware. With treatment, the muscles started to relax and, as they began to relax, the level of heartburn also decreased. Finally, I had discovered the reason for the heartburn but, unfortunately, muscles have a "memory." Muscles that have been severely cramped for five years do not relax and stay relaxed very easily. The next eight to nine years were devoted to chiropractic treatments, electrical stimulation, ultrasound, deep heat, massage, acupuncture, and stretching and strengthening exercises. Twenty years later, I am still battling the tight muscles and heartburn, and I am convinced I will continue to battle them for the rest of my life.

So what happened? Why did I tense up so severely after the death of my son? I honestly thought I was fine. I still "trusted" God, loved Him, served Him, and followed Him, remained active in the church, held leadership positions, and planned and led four short-term mission trips during that time. God slowly and lovingly showed me it was an issue of trust, or rather a lack of trust. My need to control my life and be in charge and be independent and self-sufficient kicked into hyper-drive. Although my brain continued to affirm my trust in God, my deep heart could no longer trust God to take care of me and my family. I developed a "high state of alert" and, at a subconscious level, became ever more vigilant and tense, which led to very tight muscles. Of course I could do nothing to better protect myself and my family, but being totally unaware of what was occurring in my body, mind, and heart, I had no reason to think I needed to address those feelings.

I quickly learned that trusting God with my mind was not the same thing as trusting God with my heart. I discovered that my brain had been to college but my heart was still in kindergarten. Over the ensuing years, I had to start at square one and learn what it truly meant to trust God, not just with my mind but also with my heart. My trust had been in His protection and in His ability to keep me safe and healthy. I now needed to learn how to trust God and His love, mercy, and grace—no matter what happened. I discovered that learning how to better trust God, solely through an act of the will, was impossible. "Willing myself" to trust works for my brain but not for my heart.

So, what is the answer? How can we live with hearts that truly trust God? How do we get to the place where the object of our trust is God and God alone? How do we learn to trust, not in what God will do for us, but in His love, mercy, and grace? How do we develop a true, heart level trust in God who loves us so deeply? How can we live with hearts at peace, knowing that God is with us and loves us no matter what life brings our way? We must *know* Him, really know Him, not just know *about* Him. To the degree that we truly know, at the deepest heart level, God's nature, who He is, and how deeply He loves us is the degree to which we will be able to trust Him. Reading about it, studying it, and talking about it all help but, by themselves, will not change us or lead us to trust.

How do we get to the place where we truly *know* Him? The psalmist said, "Those who know your name will trust in you, for you,

LORD, have never forsaken those who seek you" (Ps. 9:10). How can we know God's name? Who is He? How can we open the eyes of our heart to see Him as He truly is? Our brains know His name is good (Ps. 52:9). His name is Yahweh (Ps. 83:18), His name is holy and awesome (Ps. 111:9); His name is a strong tower (Prov. 18:10), and His name is Our Redeemer—the LORD Almighty (Isa. 47:4). But do our hearts truly believe this? How can we get our hearts to *believe*? How can we get our hearts to *see*?

We *know*, *believe*, and *see* when we spend regular, unhurried time in God's presence (See Chapter 6: Spending Time Alone with God). If Jesus desperately needed and desired this, it makes sense that we need it, too.

What does it mean to spend regular, unhurried time alone in God's presence? The psalmist records God's words for us when He says, "Be still and know that I am God" (Ps. 46:10). Know what? When we are alone with God, what is it we are to know? Upon what are we to focus? Our list could be endless, but here are three things to ponder.

First, I must know that God is the center of the universe—not me or my family or my stuff. Usually, I am the center of the universe, and as I come to spend time with God, I want God to join *me* and bless *me*. I want to hear what God will do for me, how He will fix my problems, how He will make my life run more smoothly. God is calling me into His presence to be with *Him*, hear from *Him*, and experience His love. As I come into His presence, He invites me to focus on the big picture.

Seeing the big picture recalibrates my heart and reminds me of who God is and who I am. Job needed that recalibration and reminder in the midst of his anger, doubt, disappointment, pain, and suffering. After Job voiced all of those emotions and more to God—God answered him. Read what God said to Job in the Old

Testament book of Job in chapters 38-41. Here is just a portion of how God responded:

> *Then the LORD answered Job from the whirlwind: "Who is this that questions my wisdom with such ignorant words? Brace yourself like a man, because I have some questions for you, and you must answer them. Where were you when I laid the foundations of the earth? Tell me, if you know so much. Who determined its dimensions and stretched out the surveying line? What supports its foundations, and who laid its cornerstone as the morning stars sang together and all the angels shouted for joy? Who kept the sea inside its boundaries as it burst from the womb, and as I clothed it with clouds and wrapped it in thick darkness? For I locked it behind barred gates, limiting its shores. I said, 'This far and no farther will you come. Here your proud waves must stop!' ... Where does light come from, and where does darkness go? Can you take each to its home? Do you know how to get there? But of course you know all this! For you were born before it was all created, and you are so very experienced!"*
>
> *Job 38:1-11, 19-21, (NLT)*

It is natural to read this and develop the impression that God was harsh and insensitive when He responded to Job. Job was suffering. Couldn't God have responded more kindly to him? But God's response was very compassionate and loving. In the midst of the chaos of Job's life, it was important for Job to recalibrate and enlarge his vision. God is God and Job is *not*. Our human brains do not know or understand a fraction of what God knows. When we come into God's presence and regularly spend unhurried time with Him, our perspective, vision, values, and priorities begin to change. To be still and to know that God is God draws us to a place where we are able to remove ourselves from the center of the universe and able to grant that seat to God.

Second, we need to know that from eternity past to eternity future, God sees the big picture with crystal clear, 20/20 vision. We do not see even one pixel's worth of the big picture. God sent Jesus, His own son, from the splendor of heaven to earth to live among us and, at the end of His time on earth, He endured horrific torture for a very specific purpose. "Because of the joy awaiting him, he [Jesus] endured the cross, disregarding its shame. Now he is seated in the place of honor beside God's throne. Think of all the hostility he endured from sinful people; then you won't become weary and give up" (Heb. 12:2b-3, NLT). Jesus clearly knew the purpose for His suffering. Unfortunately, we do not usually understand the purpose for ours. Spending time in God's presence and meditating on Jesus' pain and suffering help us trust; living in trust helps us not lose heart or give up.

Third, we need to know it gives God great pleasure when we trust Him. True trust is the ultimate form of worship. To give up our need to fully understand, to allow for divine mystery, and to trust in God's love and care no matter how bleak life appears is the best sacrifice and offering we can bring to God in worship.

What will this time with God look like when we come to "be still and know that He is God"? Our first question is usually, "how do I do it?" But the psalmist does not say, "*Do* still," he says, "*Be* still." At its root, it is not something we *do*, but it is something we allow God to do *in* us and *for* us. We show up and listen. We allow God's presence and love to fill us. We pray. But prayer is a two-way conversation; we talk *and* we listen. Praying *to* God and being *with* God are not necessarily the same thing. (See Chapter 6: "Spending

Time Alone with God" for further discussion and ideas to make this time a reality in our daily lives.)

As we draw closer to God, begin to hear His heartbeat, and begin to truly trust His love, compassion, and care, perhaps, in time, we may find we are able to agree with Habakkuk:

> *Even though the fig trees have no blossoms, and there are no grapes on the vines; even though the olive crop fails, and the fields lie empty and barren; even though the flocks die in the fields, and the cattle barns are empty, yet I will rejoice in the LORD! I will be joyful in the God of my salvation! The Sovereign LORD is my strength! He makes me as surefooted as a deer, able to tread upon the heights.*
>
> *Habakkuk 3:17-19, (NLT)*

6

Spending Time Alone with God

My wife and I are very blessed to live only a five-minute drive away from our grandchildren (nine-year-old Elijah and five-year-old Sunshine), and it is a joy to frequently spend time with them. When they come over to our house, they may stay for a few hours on a school day afternoon, spend the weekend with us, or on occasion, stay with us for a week.

How we occupy our time varies greatly from visit to visit. We eat meals, read books, play table games, play hide and seek, build motorized cars and helicopters with K'nex, or build fire engines and pirate ships with Legos. We go outside and *they* climb the rope ladder, swing in the nest swing, or rock back and forth (actually mostly wrestle) on the wide hammock. We make memories together at museums, the zoo, the Home Depot Kids' Workshop, the local beach or playground, or at McDonald's PlayPlace—the possibilities are endless. Each experience bonds us closer together and has its own nuance of fun, joy, and creating memories. But the time I treasure the most is when they first get up in the morning after having spent the night with us.

I'm usually awake by 5:30 AM and begin my devotional time in the living room in my La-Z-Boy recliner/rocker. I can almost set my watch by Elijah's footsteps in the hallway at 6:00. He wanders into the living room and plops down on the couch adjacent to my chair and, after a silent pause of five to ten seconds, begins talking as he draws from his vast, and apparently limitless, repository of knowledge and experiences using a vocabulary that is well beyond his years. He talks and I listen and, occasionally, I comment on confusing situations he has encountered or vocabulary words he has not quite mastered. It is a rich, priceless window into his soul, and I love every minute of it. Between 6:30-6:45, I hear the soft but rapid padding of bare feet coming down the hall, and rounding the corner is Sunshine, awake but still a bit sleepy. She heads over to me, pulls herself over the arm of the chair, nestles into my lap, cuddles up against me, and rocks with me but says nothing.

I respond by placing my arms around her, drawing her up close against me and, while continuing to rock, I say nothing. This is also a rich, priceless moment, and I love it. Neither child asks me for anything. During these moments, neither one of them wants me to play a game, read them a book, get them a glass of milk, or get them something to eat; we are just together, enjoying each other's company, and I love it. They have given me the no-strings-attached gift of presence, and there is nothing else that quite compares with it.

As I ponder these treasured moments with my grandchildren, my heart is drawn toward God, and I am reminded that, because I am created in His image, and therefore my need and desire for relationship and intimacy come from Him, the time I spend alone with God must also be precious to Him. I come to Him, not to ask for something or to seek His approval but just to give Him the gift of presence.

What does that actually mean, and how would I go about doing it? Unfortunately, it can be difficult to envision because my relationship with God is spiritual rather than physical, and I cannot see or touch Him. To further complicate the answer to this question, God is always with me, so I don't need to "go" somewhere to be in His presence. Perhaps I more easily perceive His presence during my morning devotional time, weekly small group gathering, or Sunday morning time of community worship. But, on the other hand, I'm just as fully in His presence while I drive my car, work, do chores around the house, eat meals, watch a movie, or listen to a concert. If this is true (and it is), then isn't my entire life a gift of presence to God? Why, then, do I, in the midst of my crazy busy life, have to set aside a special time in a special place to be alone with God every day? Is this really necessary? If I pray as I go and I listen to the Bible read from my iPad, iPod, MP3 player, phone app, or car CD player, isn't that enough—at least for most days?

It is essential to pause for a moment and, in gratitude, contemplate the privilege of God's continual presence. It is very easy to lose sight of this awesome blessing. We might take it for granted, and forget it wasn't always this way. In the time of Moses, God's presence was confined to a small room of the tabernacle (about fifteen feet square) called the Holy of Holies or the Most Holy Place. More specifically, His presence dwelt between the two cherubim on the top of the Ark of the Covenant—the sacred chest (about four feet long, two feet deep, and two feet tall) inside that room.

Although the priests were allowed to perform their duties in the Holy Place every day, a large, thick curtain separated the Holy Place from the Most Holy Place wherein only the high priest could enter, and only once a year on the Day of Atonement. The Day of Atonement was a frightening day for the high priest. Under penalty of death, the extremely detailed, meaningful, and symbolic procedure required for entering into God's presence in the Most Holy Place was to be followed to the letter of the law (read Leviticus 16 and Hebrews 9). Tradition tells us that the high priest wore bells on the lower fringes of his clothing so that the tinkling of the bells would reassure those outside the tabernacle that he was still alive and moving around, and he tied a rope around his ankle so that he could be pulled out if he should be struck dead.

There was no strolling into God's presence, reading text messages from a cell phone in one hand while holding a cup of coffee in the other. How did we get from then to now? What happened?

Jesus' death on the cross at Calvary happened. The greatest ever Day of Atonement occurred on that day when Jesus took His last breath. As He breathed His last, the tall, thick curtain that separated the Most Holy Place from the Holy Place in the temple was torn from top to bottom (Mark 15:35, Matt. 27:51), granting us the privilege to enter into His holy presence. If we accept Jesus' gift of salvation, we no longer need to follow a specific protocol to enter into His presence. He is now behind us, before us, beside us, and inside us—always.

This is wonderful news and an awesome privilege. However, if I am not careful, it can cause me to take His presence for granted and can distance me from the intimacy that gives me joy, is so essential for my spiritual health, and that brings God so much pleasure.

Since I am always in God's presence and can now pray anywhere, anytime, while doing anything, I can deceive myself into thinking it is a bit unnecessary—dare I say, almost a waste of time—to press the "pause button" on my life to spend time alone with God. Why do I need to do that? Why would I ever want to "waste" time sitting quietly with God in my living room when He is also out in my yard where I can be with Him doing something useful like mowing the lawn? Why would I "waste" time pondering and chewing over a few verses of the Bible, waiting for the Holy Spirit to open my heart to their meaning, when I could quickly head out into my busy day after reading a neatly packaged, short devotional that includes a Scripture verse with its interpretation and an insightful story to illustrate it?

Pondering all of this once again draws my heart to my relationship with my grandchildren. If we are all in the same room together—Elijah building a vehicle with Legos, Sunshine fitting together a Paw Patrol puzzle, and me catching up on emails—and we occasionally make some comments to each other about what we are each doing in our own corner, are we enjoying time together? Well, yes, of course. But, if that is the only type of "together time" we ever have, will our relationship grow? At some point, if I want to truly get to know Elijah or Sunshine at a deeper level (or want them to get to know me), I need to make eye contact with each of them and make them the prime focus of my attention. I have to drop what I am doing, leave the rest of the emails for another time, get down on the floor, and give each of them focused attention. Is it any different when it comes to building our relationship with God? I would humbly argue that it is not.

I think we can safely affirm that there has never been, nor will there ever be, another human being who has been, or will be, as close to God as Jesus was when He came to earth and lived among us. Never was there anyone else who was as aware of God's continuous presence and who ceaselessly stayed in communication with His Father. And yet, Jesus knew how much He needed to spend regular, prolonged times *alone with God*. After a long day of ministry that extended well into the evening (Mark 1:29-34), and after precious little sleep, "Very early in the morning, while it was still dark, Jesus got up, left the house and went off to a solitary place, where he prayed" (Mark 1:35). After performing an amazing miracle of feeding five thousand hungry men plus women and children, instead of hanging out with the crowd to receive affirmative and adoring "high-fives," He dismissed the crowd and "went up on a mountainside by Himself to pray. When evening came, he was there alone" (Matt. 14:23). Setting aside His need for rest and sleep, before choosing His twelve disciples, "Jesus went out to a mountainside to pray, and spent the night praying to God" (Luke 6:12). If Jesus needed that, wouldn't I also need it?

If we are to spend one-on-one quality time with God—where He is the sole focus of our attention—what do we do? What will that time look like? Should we follow some sort of patterned routine? Is there a list of essential elements we should carefully include?

Thomas Keating boiled it down to: "The only way to fail in prayer is not to show up."[1] Perhaps the only essential element is to quit talking about it and actually do it. We are giving God the gift of presence, and He loves it when He is the prime focus of our attention—no matter what elements we include. As A. W. Tozer states, "God waits to be wanted."[2]

We listen, we talk, and we read His written Word. We praise, we worship, we confess, we meditate, we ponder, we reflect, and we share our heart. We come to God in reverence and awe, but with boldness and confidence. We come to Him, the King of kings and the Lord of lords. We come to Him, the Almighty God who created the universe. We come to Him, the one who knows everything—from eternity past to eternity future. We come to Him, our Shepherd. We come to Him, our Abba Father—Daddy. We come to Him as a beloved bride comes before her loving Bridegroom. We come before Him, knowing He delights in us. We come to give Him our focused, undivided attention. We come for the express purpose of being with Him—spending time with Him. We come into His presence to *be*, not to *do*.

Having said all that, there are things we "do," but those are secondary to giving Him the gift of our presence, our full attention, and our love. This distinction and heart-level perspective is crucial; otherwise, anything we "do" will quickly become performance-based rote, duty, and boredom and rapidly fall into heart-numbing ruts—or we'll just quit.

What might occur during this time with God? Myriads of books have been written in an attempt to help us achieve the "proper goals" so that "God will be pleased with us," we will grow spiritually, and we will be "rewarded" with answers to our prayers. With so much written on this topic, how can one short chapter in this book possibly tell us anything new? Primarily, I would encourage us not to look for new truths or techniques, but to develop a new approach to our time alone with God—develop a new way of *seeing*.

Yes, there are principles to learn and implement, but achieving a mastery of them is not what will develop greater intimacy with God. Intimacy with God will blossom when we learn to rest in God's presence, truly *know* Him (not just know *about* Him), trust Him, enjoy Him, and, at the heart level, become convinced that we are His beloved children.

With this perspective and approach as our foundation, I briefly want to examine some of the ingredients we might incorporate into our time with God. They are worship, prayer, Bible reading, meditation, and journaling. In reality, all these elements intermingle, more or less occur simultaneously, and cannot properly be teased apart; but, for purposes of discussion, we will explore them separately. In our everyday lives, it is usually difficult to turn the focus of our minds and hearts toward God and away from the duties, frustrations, and worries of the day. Therefore, it is helpful at the outset to spend a few minutes sitting still, in silence, to let the "dust settle," and allow our blood pressure, pulse rate, and breathing rate to calm down a bit.

WORSHIP

"O Lord, you are my God; I will exalt you and praise your name, for in perfect faithfulness you have done marvelous things, things planned long ago" (Isa. 25:1). From Genesis to Revelation, God's Word motivates and inspires us to worship Him because God deserves our worship and, when we worship, we are drawn to the heart of God. Engaging our physical bodies in the act of worship can frequently assist our minds and hearts in focusing on God. Since we are alone, we need not concern ourselves with what others might think. We can remove our shoes to acknowledge we are on holy ground, we can stand in reverence, kneel in humility, raise our hands in praise, lie prostrate on the floor in contrition, open our hands and face them upward to receive God's blessing, sing out loud, read Scripture out loud—or do none of these. We do that which helps us focus on God and, with grateful hearts, declare the truths of His majesty, power, mercy, grace, and love.

It is helpful to realize that, as we begin to worship, a steady stream of unrelated thoughts will attempt to flood our minds. It may sound something like this: "Oh no, I forgot my computer anti-virus needs to be updated today; I really should stop and do that right now. I can't believe how insensitive my friend was yesterday; why did he treat me so poorly? Why doesn't anyone RSVP for the upcoming family dinner? They never respond; it's so frustrating. How will we know how much food to prepare? Why did I get angry at my wife over such an insignificant issue? When will I ever learn? There are so many projects to do around the house when I get home from work today. I better stop now and make a list, so I don't forget something important. Oh dear, I forgot, the gas tank in the car is nearly empty; I'll have to leave the house early this morning so I can stop and fill it up on the way to work. Let's see, what time is it? Yikes! I better get going now. Sorry God, I'll try again tomorrow."

I've found it helpful to have a pen and a pad of paper beside me so I can jot down my thoughts as they come to mind. I can then return to worship without "fear" that I will forget them.

When we allow God to orchestrate our thoughts and the direction of our worship, He will bring words to mind that we can use to worship Him. They may be words from a song or a hymn that we allow to flood our hearts. We can sing it or just slowly savor the words and allow them to penetrate our souls. He may bring a Bible verse, phrase, or word to mind that we can ponder, then turn it into a prayer of praise. He may remind us of a Bible story or brief scenario upon which we can reflect. We can then place ourselves in the story and allow it to amaze us with the awesomeness of God and how He has worked among His people in the past. We don't just think about it for a second or two then quickly move on to something else. We bathe in it, soak in it, ponder it, and then, dropping to our knees in worship, shake our heads in wonder and awe.

As God brings to mind His creation, we may form a mental picture of floating out in space somewhere watching as—at God's command—light suddenly explodes into the universe at the speed of 186,000 miles a second while gazillions of stars instantly appear and organize into galaxies. As we continue to watch, planets appear and rotate around a star. As one planet bursts into color, we see a dazzling variety of animals running, birds flying, and fish swimming. We turn our eyes from the planet and look out into billions of light-years of space but see no end to the universe. We stay with this mental image until we are drawn to worship the majesty and glory of God.

We can stand at the side of the Red Sea and let our mouths drop open as God parts the water so we can all cross on dry ground. We can stand in the open field and watch a chariot of fire suddenly whisk Elijah off to only God knows where. Or, we can sit and cry at the foot of the cross as we watch Jesus suffer in agony—for us. We can quietly listen as God brings to mind a truth about Himself such as His gentleness, forgiveness, tenderness, or kindness, and then chew on it until it turns our hearts to worship. These examples are only a microscopic sample of what might transpire in our time of worship with God. Each day will be different as we wait patiently in the stillness of God's presence.

PRAYER

In his letter to the church in Philippi, the apostle Paul introduces two facets of prayer. "Do not be anxious about anything, but in everything, by prayer and petition with thanksgiving, present your requests to God" (Phil. 4:6). The Greek word that is translated as "petition," means to ask for stuff—to make our needs known to God.[3] However, the word "prayer" is a more sacred word.[4] Literally it means the "prayer *of* God."[5] This is the word used by the gospel writers to describe Jesus when He prayed all night (see above).

Most of us know how to bring our worries before God, but we often struggle with listening to God and praying His heart. A wonderful way to do this is to pray God's words from Scripture. Please do not misunderstand. God loves it when we present our requests to Him; but a close, intimate relationship with Him involves more than pleading for a divine solution to our problems. It gives God great pleasure when we set our concerns aside, and come just to *be* with Him.

The psalmist says, "But I have calmed and quieted my soul, like a weaned child with its mother; like a weaned child is my soul within me" (Ps. 131:2, ESV). We come into God's presence to be with Him, not just to request something. Weaned children no longer focus on feeding at their mother's breast; they can be content to be with her and enjoy her company, warmth, and presence. True prayer involves a new way of seeing ourselves, seeing God, and seeing how He desires to interrelate with us. Mother Teresa said, "Prayer is not asking. Prayer is putting oneself in the hands of God, at His disposition, and listening to His voice in the depth of our hearts."[6]

Eugene Peterson suggests that, "Prayer is the way we work our way out of the comfortable but cramped world of self into the self-denying but spacious world of God."[7] In prayer, we not only present our urgent pleas, but we listen and hear God's heart. We discover His desires for our lives and how much He loves us.

BIBLE READING

"All Scripture is inspired by God and is useful to teach us what is true and to make us realize what is wrong in our lives. It corrects us when we are wrong and teaches us to do what is right. God uses it to prepare and equip his people to do every good work" (2 Tim. 3:16-17, NLT). "For the word of God is alive and powerful. It is sharper than the sharpest two-edged sword, cutting between soul and spirit, between joint and marrow. It exposes our innermost thoughts and desires" (Heb. 4:12, NLT).

Dr. Mulholland states, "In our spiritual reading of scripture we become available to God, open to the penetration of God's living Word, and responsive to the shaping of God's will for our wholeness and life."[8]

We come to spend time with, and make ourselves available to, God, and allow Him to speak to our hearts through His written Word. We come to encounter a Person, not a Book. Our purpose for reading is not to fill our heads with interesting information like when we read an encyclopedia. Or, as Eugene Peterson quips, like when we remove our Bible from the shelf where we stored it thinking "that we are honoring it by consulting it from time to time as an indispensable reference work."[9]

We come to the scriptures with the expectation that God will meet us, converse with us, and lovingly transform us. As Karl Rahner says, "Some things are understood not by grasping but by allowing oneself to be grasped."[10]

Our predominant focus is not to learn the "correct" way of reading to make sure we "get something out of it." We need to read in such a way that God's Word can shape and change us. The strategy or process we use will be different from that used by others and will change as we periodically search for new methods (there are many books that offer suggestions) to help us focus and open our hearts to God's working within us.

Lectio Divina or "divine reading" is a form of contemplative reading and prayer that has been used by believers for centuries. It consists of four parts. The titles, as well as the explanation of what occurs in each of these four parts, vary somewhat according to the author who explains them. Basically, we read a short portion of scripture slowly and thoughtfully four times. The first time we read, we simply listen. The second time we read, we ask God how the passage touches our lives. The third time we read, we ask God how to apply the truths to our lives. The fourth time we read, we remain quiet, meditate, and allow God to minister to our hearts. A more simplified version of a Lectio Divina explanation can be found in a wonderful devotional, *Be Still and Know that I am God,* compiled by Amy and Judge Reinhold,[11] and a more thorough explanation can be found in Ruth Haley Barton's life-changing book, *Sacred Rhythms.*[12]

MEDITATION

Meditation is perhaps one of the most misunderstood aspects of our Christian life. When mentioned, many followers of Jesus raise their eyebrows, become angry, or declare it to be dangerous. Why would this be? Some relate it to "transcendental meditation," a "New Age Movement" practice, or the equivalent of a Buddhist-encouraged "emptying of the mind." Others declare it to be dangerous because they feel it places us in a position where Satan or his demons can speak to us and deceive us into believing it came from God. Why would meditation cause these concerns? Why would a practice God commanded to Joshua, about 3400 years ago, become so maligned now in the twenty-first century?

Dallas Willard argues that just because authentic, Spirit-led meditation has been counterfeited, "It would be strange if we came to shun the genuine simply because it resembled the counterfeit."[13] The Buddhist religion began somewhere between the sixth and fourth centuries B.C.[14] (less than 2600 years ago), Transcendentalism began in the 1820s-1830s[15] (less than 200 years ago), and the New Age Movement began in the 1970s[16] (50 years ago).

Since God told Joshua nearly 1000 years before Buddhism developed to meditate twice a day, shouldn't it be the reverse, where those in Buddhism, Transcendentalism, and the New Age Movement would be the ones to raise their eyebrows, become angry, and declare dangerous a practice commanded by the Jewish God? And where do we get the idea that the devil will attempt to deceive us during meditation but does not attempt to influence us during the rest of the day? Every minute of every day, the devil bombards us with accusations, lies, and temptations. Do we blindly listen and obey them? Of course not. We learn to hear and recognize God's voice. We learn how to distinguish God's voice from the voice of the enemy of our souls, who frequently poses as an angel of light to deceive and destroy us. In speaking of a true shepherd, Jesus says, "He calls his own sheep by name and leads them out. When he has brought out all his own, he goes on ahead of them, and his sheep follow him because they know his voice" (John 10:3b-4). Jesus is our Good Shepherd, and as we follow Him, we also know His voice. Why would it be that we can recognize the voice of God speaking and distinguish it from the voice of the stranger and thief (John 10: 4, 8-10) all throughout the day but are unable to do so during our times alone with God as we meditate on His greatness and love?

After the people mourned Moses' death, God appointed Joshua to lead them on the new phase of their journey to cross the Jordan

River and enter the Promised Land. It was not easy to follow in the footsteps of Moses—their beloved, wise leader—and Joshua was understandably anxious. Three times, God encouraged Joshua to be strong and courageous and then gave him the secret to success in his new position of leadership. God commanded him, "Do not let this Book of the Law depart from your mouth; meditate on it day and night, so that you may be careful to do everything written in it. Then you will be prosperous and successful" (Josh. 1:8). Joshua would be able to follow and obey God's laws if he meditated on them every morning and night. Prosperity and success—as God defined it—would become a reality to Joshua if he obeyed; and, with God's strength, obedience was possible if, through meditation, Joshua developed a thorough, heart-level knowledge of God's law.

What did God mean when He told Joshua to meditate? The Hebrew word that is translated as "meditate" means "the act of thoughtful deliberation with the implication of speaking to oneself."[17] We tell ourselves the truth, we go over it again, we rehearse it, we ponder it, we think deeply about it to the point of being "lost in thought," we soak in it, and we marinate in it. It is like chewing our food very slowly or, better yet, like a cow chewing its cud. The cow ruminates to better digest and absorb all the nutrients from its food. It chews and chews and eventually swallows, but, later, it regurgitates its food and chews some more. We do the same with God's Word when we meditate. The psalmist tells us we meditate on God's Word day and night because it is our delight (Ps. 1:2).

Some followers of Jesus use the argument that meditation is only talked about in the Old Testament and that it was no longer a discipline in the early church, but there are Greek words in the New Testament such as "consider" (Heb. 12:3), "ponder" (Luke 2:19), or "reflect on" (2 Tim. 2:7) that mean the same thing as meditation. Clearly, the instruction to focus our complete, prolonged, and intense attention on God's Word occurs throughout the entire

Bible. The truths of God's Word will never grow in our hearts if they blow in one ear and out the other. We can't just spend five to ten minutes in the morning reading a quick devotional and then get on with our day if God's Word is to inform and change our lives. We must meditate, ponder, consider, and reflect on what we read if we want to experience spiritual growth and intimacy with God.

As the old saying goes: "We think about what we think about." Think about it! I'm sure we all experience times when the details and the steps to complete a project at work or at home consume our lives. During those times, when we're not actively engaged in a specific task, we find our thoughts drawn to that project because the details have been turning around and around in our brains so often. The same can happen in our spiritual lives. When we fill our minds with a few verses of Scripture in the morning, carefully meditate on them, and allow them to soak into our hearts, those thoughts will then resurface later so that we can continue to chew on them throughout the day.

JOURNALING

At the conclusion of a particularly difficult battle against the Amalekites, using a uniquely designed strategy for victory, God told Moses to "Write this on a scroll as something to be remembered" (Exod. 17: 14a). One of the best ways to remember something is to write it down. We write down God's insights, how He moves in our lives, how He fights our battles, and the impact it all has on our minds and hearts. Recording the details is an excellent way to remember each event, and can become a great source of blessing when we reread it next week, next month, or even years later. Remembering what God has done—for us, in us, and through us—is a crucial component of growing in our intimacy with Him (See Chapter 1: "Remembering God's Acts of Grace").

Many believe they dislike journaling simply because they have not tried it. I was one of those people. I always felt it was a waste of time to record my thoughts and prayers and God's insights. It is certainly a lot quicker to just think about something than it is to take the time to write it down. But journaling doesn't just help us remember in the future; it helps us grow right now in the present because we greatly benefit when we say something out loud or when we write it down.

I love Rick Warren's maxim: "Thoughts become disentangled when they pass between our lips or fingertips."[18] I can think I have a clear sense of what God is saying to me as I read a portion of scripture, but when I begin to write it down, I realize my thoughts aren't as well developed as I presumed. As I begin to write, my thoughts flow, and I am often amazed at how God speaks through my heart and out through my pen.

LESSONS FROM MY "TIME ALONE WITH GOD" JOURNEY

After the death of our son Ben in November 1992, my response to life changed dramatically (See Chapters 4 and 5: "Grieving with Hope" and "Trusting God"). Although at the time, I was largely unaware of all that was transpiring in my heart (and subsequently also in my physical body), I slowly developed a "high state of alert." I subconsciously reasoned that if God could no longer be trusted to protect my family and me, I now had to be the protector. My brain did not believe this, nor would I, even remotely state it out loud, but, now, in retrospect, I can sadly see that my heart embraced it. This "high state of alert" resulted in epinephrine release, increased heart rate, tenseness, muscle cramping, heartburn, and a depletion of my brain serotonin levels—all physically damaging to my body, mind, and soul. Over the years, I slowly developed a mild depression and anxiety that gradually impacted my confidence at work. I began to second-guess decisions I made on the job and would then worry about them while at home—especially at night. Although I never had any panic attacks, my increasing anxiety level and occasional thoughts of "impending doom" were taking their toll on me, and I came to the place of realizing I could not continue to live like that. Even though I frequently prayed for inner peace, it remained elusive.

I cannot recall what prompted me to begin reading books written by Henri Nouwen, Breenan Manning, Ken Gire, and others. But, as I did, over time, the Holy Spirit slowly worked in my heart and drew me to an early morning, daily, prolonged time alone with God—referred to in the books as a time of silence and solitude. As encouraged by the authors and as discussed above, I then wrote down the thoughts and insights God gave me.

I began this time alone with God on August 23, 2006, and have been doing it every day since (now over fourteen years). Did it make a difference? Is it still making a difference? Did I begin to experience peace in my mind and heart? Yes, but I now know those are the wrong questions to ask. Only three days into this new way of life, on August 26, as I was once again pleading for peace, I powerfully sensed God saying to me: "Don't be hungry for a heart that is at peace, be hungry for Me." That was the first lesson I discovered in this new adventure with God. I quickly became aware that the reason I wanted to spend time with God every morning was not because I desired to be in the presence of, and develop an intimate relationship with, the God of the universe who loved me and sent Jesus to die for me, but for what He could *do* for me. I desperately wanted peace! My subconscious thoughts went something like this: "If I bring Him pleasure by spending time with Him, then He will reward my prayers and give me peace." Thus began the winding, turning, and, at times, steep path toward learning how to *be* with God, getting to know Him (not just know about Him), taking delight in His presence, and loving Him for the marvelous God that He is—even if I never experienced any peace.

Henri Nouwen said it would take nine months of spending daily time alone with God to truly be able to settle my thoughts, tune out the distractions, and quiet my heart so I could hear God's still small voice.[19] When I read that comment fourteen years ago, my immediate response was to groan in despair and think, "You've got to be kidding! It's going to take that long?"

By the end of May 2007, as the nine months drew to a close, my response turned to disbelief and discouragement as I thought, "How in the world did Nouwen get to that place in only nine months?" Now, fourteen years later, I still struggle with truly calming my heart, settling my thoughts, tuning out the distractions, and hearing His still small voice. I still ask myself, on occasion, "Am I doing this whole thing, right?" For me, that has been lesson number two. I will never learn how to *do* it "correctly" so that it all *works* the way it is "supposed to" because it isn't about *doing*, getting something to *work*, learning the correct pattern to follow, or mastering the seven foolproof steps that, if followed, will ensure intimacy with God and consistently answered prayer (as some books promise us). It is about developing a love relationship, getting to know God's desires, motives, purposes, and values, and allowing them to gradually but consistently soak deeply into my heart so that they become my desires, motives, purposes, and values.

The third lesson I learned is that only God can grow and change me. In his gospel, Mark records Jesus' words.

> *This is what the kingdom of God is like. A man scatters seed on the ground. Night and day, whether he sleeps or gets up, the seed sprouts and grows,* **though he does not know how.** **All by itself** *the soil produces grain—first the stalk, then the head, then the*

*full kernel in the head. As soon as the grain is ripe,
he puts the sickle to it, because the harvest has come.
(emphasis mine).*

Mark 4:26-29

Farmers do not kneel down in the earth and pick open the seeds and tease out a stem and a leaf, nor do they use some sort of stretching rack to elongate the stems to make them taller. Farmers do nothing to *cause* the plants to grow.

Wait a minute, is that true? Farmers are certainly busy doing something! What is it? I have an air-tight pail filled with grass seeds that have been in my shed for over two years. They are unchanged from the day I bought them. Are they dead? Did I pay good money for seeds that are worthless? No, those seeds will remain unchanged—for years to come—until I provide the proper environment for their growth. If I take them out of the pail, place them in warm, moist, enriched soil where they will receive sunlight, they will quickly begin to thrive. So it is with me. When I spend time alone with God, my focus is not on changing or growing my heart—that is God's task. My focus is on providing the warm, moist, nutrient-rich environment in which God can work in me so that I sprout, grow, mature, and bear fruit. Instead of asking if I am doing what I need to do to grow, my question now becomes, "Am I doing what I need to do to provide a fertile environment for growth?"

The fourth lesson I've learned is that this time with God cannot be rushed. It takes time to quiet my heart, tune out the distractions and the loud voices in my mind and heart, turn my heart to worship, ponder what God is saying through His Word, and write down what I hear. Five minutes is insufficient if I want to truly encounter God. Some days are rushed and five or ten minutes is all that is available (and that is certainly better than zero minutes), but my ongoing intent is to carve out unhurried time to be with God every day.

I've also learned (lesson five) that setting aside a more prolonged time to be alone with God is of great value. In October 2006, two months after the start of my new journey, I set aside a weekend for a personal silence and solitude retreat and have repeated that numerous times over the last fourteen years. I've used the Abbey of the Genesee[20] because it is not far from my home. This allows me forty-eight hours away from the routines of life to focus on God. These weekends have been invaluable for recharging my batteries and replenishing my emotional tank. They help me rediscover the big picture of who God is, who I am, and how we walk this life together. They allow the "dust to settle" in my brain and refresh, restore, recalibrate, and transform my heart. They are a time to reboot, press the reset button on my priorities, values, and perspectives, and return all my defaults back to their proper God-desired positions. And, just as important, as Brennan Manning adds, "God likes it when I show up."[21]

> *Be still and know that I am God; I will be exalted among the nations, I will be exalted in the earth.*
> *Psalm 46:10*

> *Be still before the Lord and wait patiently for him.*
> *Psalm 37:7a*

> *The Lord is in his holy temple; let all the earth be silent before him.*
> *Habakkuk 2:20*

> *Be silent before the Sovereign Lord, for the day of the Lord is near.*
> *Zephaniah 1:7*

As the deer pants for streams of water, so my soul pants
for you, O God. My soul thirsts for God, for the living
God. When can I go and meet with God?

Psalm 42:1-2

When can we go and meet with God? Today would be
wonderful!

7

Living with a Grateful Heart

What does it mean to have a grateful heart? When God answers our prayers, does it elicit a true heart level gratitude or only a thankful sense of relief that we can now put that problem behind us? Does anything about us change as a result of that answered prayer, or do we merely respond with a quick "thank you, "catch you later, God," and then return to our busy lives? Do we find it challenging to be grateful to God when He answers our prayers for "smaller concerns" but never answers our prayers for those struggles that are more difficult to endure?

Why would one man who experiences Jesus' healing power stop, praise, and worship God from a deep heart of gratitude and then, in humility, throw himself at Jesus' feet while nine others who experience the exact same miracle breathe a sigh of relief that their problem is solved and walk away from Jesus without so much as a *thank you*? Of course, there may be many reasons, but one reason to ponder is that one man sees with the eyes of his heart while the other nine do not. There is nothing wrong with their physical vision. All ten physically see the miraculous answer to their prayers, but only one is grateful. Luke tells us the story,

Now on his way to Jerusalem, Jesus traveled along the border between Samaria and Galilee. As he was

> *going into a village, ten men who had leprosy met*
> *him. They stood at a distance and called out in a loud*
> *voice, "Jesus, Master, have pity on us!" When he saw*
> *them, he said, "Go, show yourselves to the priests."*
> *And as they went, they were cleansed. One of them,*
> *when he saw he was healed, came back, praising God*
> *in a loud voice. He threw himself at Jesus' feet and*
> *thanked him—and he was a Samaritan. Jesus asked,*
> *"Were not all ten cleansed? Where are the other nine?*
> *Has no one returned to give praise to God except this*
> *foreigner?" Then he said to him, "Rise and go; your*
> *faith has made you well."*
>
> *Luke 17:11-19*

While Jesus was approaching the outskirts of a village, ten men with leprosy called out to Him from a distance. The Greek word that is translated as "leprosy" does not refer just to the disease we know today as Hanson's Disease, but is a generic word that can refer to various possible skin conditions. It does not matter what they are; what matters is that they are all contagious. A priest has examined them and told them they must leave their homes, their jobs, their families, and their communities, and they must live outside the town, well away from others.

Think of the ramifications of this grim pronouncement given by the priest. If a man has no son to run the farm or whatever business he has, his wife and children will become destitute. If one of these men is a day laborer, then his wife and children will also become destitute. In addition to the financial considerations, think also of the emotional impact of being removed from society. These men can no longer have any contact with their family; they cannot attend community celebrations, synagogue services, weddings, or funerals.

The ramifications are so enormous that it is probably impossible for us to truly understand the impact this disease has on their lives.

The author of the book of Leviticus tells us what they are to do after the diagnosis is made.

> *Those who suffer from a serious skin disease must tear their clothing and leave their hair uncombed. They must cover their mouth and call out, 'Unclean! Unclean!' As long as the serious disease lasts, they will be ceremonially unclean. They must live in isolation in their place outside the camp.*
> *Leviticus 13:45-46, (NLT)*

These ten men are most likely living together in a cave, supporting each other as best as they can. No wonder they shout to Jesus for mercy (pity). Luke says they are "[calling] out in a loud voice" or "crying out." In the Greek, this phrase is one word and means to cry out loudly or to shout loudly.[1] They are screaming in order to be clearly heard. Also, the word here is singular, not plural, which tells us that all ten men are crying out loudly as one voice. Are they pleading for alms (food or money) as they normally do whenever anyone passes them by? Most likely not. They know Jesus' name and, most likely, have heard of Him and of His healing powers. They also call Him "Master," which is a term the gospel writers usually use only when they describe how the disciples refer to Jesus. These ten men clearly want Jesus to heal them—and they are desperate.

There are profound benefits to their lives if their skin is healed, and they dream of those benefits every day. They would be able to return to their families and be able to hug their wives, children, and grandchildren. They would be able to go back to work and support themselves and their families. They would be able to take part in the community activities and celebrations and attend the synagogue and other religious activities. Yes, they are crying out loudly—as one voice—for mercy. "Jesus have pity on us!" Luke tells us that Jesus sees these ten lepers. Luke did not need to include this phrase; everyone could see them and hear them quite well. That fact was obvious. Luke clearly had more in mind here when he said that *Jesus sees them*. In other stories, Jesus frequently comments on those who can see and those who cannot, and He isn't usually referring to physical eyesight. There is seeing with our physical eyes and there is seeing with our hearts, and there is a vast difference between them.

True seeing, with both our physical eyes and our hearts, leads us to do something about what we see. Jesus "sees" the opportunity to be merciful to ten hurting men. This is not just saying "yes" to men who want dermatological healing. This leprosy does not affect just the men's skin; it affects their entire being, their entire existence, and Jesus sees that.

Charles-François-Bienvenu Myriel—referred to as Bishop Myriel or Monseigneur Bienvenu—sees that when he encounters Jean Valjean in the 1862 French novel *Les Miserables* written by Victor Hugo. *Les Miserables*, considered one of the greatest novels of the nineteenth century, covers a twenty-year period, leading up to the 1832 June rebellion. Multiple musicals, plays, movies, and radio broadcasts have been created in an attempt to reenact this novel.

Jean Valjean spent nineteen years in hard labor prison—five years for stealing bread for his starving sister and her children and fourteen years as punishment for his numerous escape attempts. After release, he was required to carry a yellow passport so everyone knew he was an ex-convict. No one gave him a meal, took him in for the night, or gave him a job. All those he encountered believed the same thing, "Once a thief, always a thief."

Finally, late one evening, Jean Valjean stumbled across a monastery and Bishop Myriel invited him in for dinner and a warm bed for the night. While everyone was fast asleep, Jean got up, stole the priest's silver, and ran off into the night. The law enforcement authorities quickly caught him and triumphantly dragged him back to the monastery. However, after thanking the authorities for their speedy arrest, Bishop Myriel tells them they could release him and set him free because he had given Jean the silver as a gift. The bishop then chides Jean, in front of the authorities, for leaving in such a hurry that he forgot to take the silver candlesticks as well. That unimaginable act of kindness and forgiveness utterly and completely changed Jean's life. The bishop did not see a smelly, dirty, unkempt, predictable thief, but saw beneath all of that and, seeing Jean with the eyes of his heart, responded with mercy and pity.

To truly "see" is to look past just the physically visible exterior shell and, seeing as God sees, act in response to what we see. To truly see is to view God at work in the situation and to join Him in ministering to others. Jesus "sees" the ten men, but He doesn't just see ten cases of leprosy that need to be healed. He doesn't just see ten requests for something He can supply. He sees ten desperately hurting and discouraged men who long to return to their families and, because He "sees," He responds with mercy.

Jesus does not instantly heal them, but tells them to go and show themselves to the priests. In addition to their many other duties, the priests serve as "skin inspectors." They are not doctors or those who perform healings; they merely inspect and banish people from the community if they have a contagious disease or bring them back into the community when they are healed. As the ten men walk, as they obey Jesus, they are totally cleansed of their skin disease. It takes faith to walk away from Jesus. Jesus is the source of their healing and they would prefer not to leave Jesus until their skin is restored. However, they trust Jesus, walk away, and, after making a quick survey of their body parts, rejoice in the discovery that their skin is now healthy. But, in the midst of all their relief and joy, one man's response is very different. What distinguishes that one man from the other nine?

Luke says the one man "saw he was healed." Don't the other nine also see they are healed? Aren't all ten jumping up and down greatly relieved that Jesus healed them, that their suffering is over, and that they can now return to their families? They must be saying, "Yes! This is awesome! I can't wait to hug my wife! I can't wait to get back to work!" But though they physically see their healthy skin, they don't truly see. They don't see with the eyes of their hearts. They miss the true source of their healing, and they lack the humility to appreciate how undeserving they are. Perhaps, whether conscious or not, they feel they deserve to be healed. They may be thinking, "I didn't deserve to get leprosy in the first place. God allowed me to get this terrible disease; the least He can do is heal me. Good, now it's gone. Now I can get on with my life. I'm a good person and, frankly, I deserve to be healed."

It is difficult to truly be grateful when we don't have a humble heart toward God. Humility toward God means we have a deep realization of our unworthiness to receive God's marvelous grace. Grace is undeserved. Mercy is undeserved. If we can't see with the eyes of our hearts, we can't genuinely be grateful. Sure, we might voice a quick *thank you* or have a momentary sense of relief that we no longer need to deal with our problem, but we will not experience true gratitude. We say to ourselves, "I only received what I deserved. God owed me that. I'm a good person. I do a lot of good stuff for God." To be grateful is to recognize and truly know—a deep, heart level knowing—that our lives have been touched by God's mercy, love, and grace.

While nine men headed to the priest to have their healthy skin documented, so they can get on with their lives, one man ran back to Jesus with a profoundly grateful heart. His grateful heart rose up into his vocal cords and he screamed his praise to God. In the Greek, "loud voice" means "exceedingly great."[2]

If we are to really understand what is going on in this story, we must place ourselves in the crowd and, in our imagination, watch this man as he ran back to Jesus. He was yelling, he was shouting, he was screaming his praise to God. And in his enthusiastic, unabated praise to God, he threw himself at Jesus' feet.

Can you picture this? What do you think? A bit undignified? A bit unsophisticated? A bit uncalled for? Does he need to restrain his emotions a bit? Wouldn't a simple heartfelt "thank you" suffice? Our response to these questions gives us a window into our own heart of gratitude to God. People who truly see are filled with gratitude and then fall to their knees in worship. As they worship in gratitude, their hearts are changed. Changed hearts lead to changed lives that are lived with new motives, values, and priorities.

Luke then adds, "Oh, by the way, one more thing—he's a Samaritan." A muffled gasp can be heard from the crowd as they think, "What?" Samaritans are regarded as unclean. This man is "doubly unclean." He's a Samaritan *and* he has leprosy.

Samaritans were descendants of the mixed marriages that resulted from the settlement of Assyrian people into Israel after most of the Jewish people were removed from Israel and taken into captivity when the northern kingdom fell to Assyria.[3] The Jewish people's distain for the Samaritans went well beyond prejudice—it was all-out hatred. It is the Samaritan, the "foreigner," the despised one who truly sees and responds with a heart of gratitude. Jesus tells him, "Rise and go; your faith has made you well." Your faith has saved you, rescued you, delivered you. What did Jesus mean? In response to their faith, all ten lepers are healed as they leave Jesus and make their way to the priest. Here, Jesus means something more than physical healing; Jesus refers to the man's spiritual healing. The

Samaritan truly sees who Jesus is and responds to His love, mercy, and grace.

Westermann asks, "Why do some encounter God in their healing, while others do not?"[4]

Why is it that the Samaritan "sees" and the other nine do not? What is the difference between those who are grateful and those who are only relieved that their suffering is behind them? A grateful heart can see. A grateful heart reveals a heart of humility toward God and is able to see that we don't deserve what God has done for us; a grateful heart sees it is God's grace, God's mercy, and God's love.

The main point of the story is not the miraculous healing of the ten men with leprosy, but what they do as a result of their healing. What does Jesus do when He sees the men with diseased skin? He has compassion. What does Bishop Myriel do when he sees a dangerous convict who has obviously not broken his thieving habit? He forgives. What does the Samaritan, healed of leprosy, do when he sees he is healed? He sees, not just his clear skin, but that it was God who healed him through Jesus' power, and he worships with a deep heart of gratitude. What does Jean Valjean do when he sees the priest's forgiveness, compassion, and generosity? He is undone. He stumbles to the chapel and drops to his knees in disbelief. There is nothing in his brain or heart that can process what has just happened to him.

The awareness of his sin, and his profound gratitude to the bishop for his kindness, love, mercy, and forgiveness, turns every cell in his heart upside down. His life is utterly and completely transformed. Not only does he leave his life of theft and brutality, but he reaches out to help and care for all those around him. What do the nine men do when their physical eyes see that Jesus has answered their cry for mercy? They keep right on walking and go on with their lives, relieved that they no longer have leprosy.

What about us? What do we see, and what do we do when we see? It depends a great deal on whether we see only with our physical eyes or if we also see with the eyes of our hearts. The first "see" here in Luke's story is the ability to see those around us at a deeper level than just their superficial appearance and be able to recognize their true needs. Do we see a frustrating coworker, or do we see a coworker who lives with constant pain? Do we see an annoyingly withdrawn neighbor, or do we see a neighbor who has just been told he has terminal cancer? Do we see an immigrant as someone who is difficult to communicate with due to a language barrier, or do we see her as someone who has had a hard life, is far from home, and is separated from her family?

The second "see" in Luke's story gets to the heart of the story and how we see God when He meets our needs. In relief, do we say a quick "thank you" and go right on with our lives as usual, or do we pause, drop to our knees in worship, and, in gratitude, live a life now focused on bringing Him pleasure? Culpepper says, "For those who have become aware of God's grace, all of life is infused with a sense of gratitude, and each encounter becomes an opportunity to see and to respond in the spirit of the grateful leper."[5] Are we able to truly see God's grace when He pours it out over us, and does it move us to gratitude?

EXPERIENCING GRATITUDE

As a result of the 2008-2009 recession, after working nearly thirty-two years as a Pediatric Physician Assistant, on June 26, 2009, I joined the ranks of the unemployed. With less and less to keep me busy in a dwindling pediatric clinic, I knew for ten months that it was only a matter of time before I would lose my job. When the manager came into my office that fateful Friday afternoon, I was not surprised. What did surprise me, however, was that, instead of anxiety, resentment, or anger, my immediate reaction was one of relief—like I'd been set free from bondage—and gratitude to God for the gift He had given me. More and more, my job had become a source of frustration and stress. But, because of concern about income and medical insurance, I refused to quit. God gave me a gift and took my stressful job away from me.

I felt like a new chapter in my life had begun, but what would it look like, where would it lead me, how would I get there, and where would we get money for the transition period? God reassured me that, even though it felt like I was walking through a dense forest in the dark of night, He was holding my hand and that which looked like a dense, dark, forest to me was bright daylight to Him. Re-reading my journal—from my early morning devotional time before heading into work that life-changing day—was clear evidence God knew what was to transpire later that day and had prepared me for it. If He knew the future of that day, He certainly knew the rest of my future and could reliably guide me into it. That morning I sensed God was saying, "Be still and know that I am God. Do not worry, do not fret. Be strong and courageous. I am with you, be not afraid, I am your God. You are not alone. Trust Me. Lean on Me."[6] After reading Colossians 1:11, I wrote, "May this verse be true of me! Strengthen me in accordance with your *glorious might* so that I can have great endurance and patience. Your power, infused into me, is for a purpose ... It is power I will need to survive! I am going to need *great* endurance and patience ... give me that endurance and patience for today."[7] I had no idea what the day would bring as I wrote, but God did! What a blessing that God prepared me for what was to occur that afternoon.

I was blessed with three months' severance pay and medical insurance, and I quickly applied for unemployment insurance and COBRA medical insurance that would begin in October. Now what? A thirty-two year career as a PA was a bit tough to walk away from, but I distinctly felt I was not to look for another PA job. If not, then what? What should I do next? Go back to school? If so, to study what? And, how would I pay for it? I had no idea!

However, only a few days passed before my heart quickly drew me toward that for which God had been preparing me for many years—full-time ministry.

My wife, Cheryl, asked me, "If money wasn't a concern, what would you do?"

I immediately responded, "I'd go to seminary." It just popped out of my mouth before I hardly even processed the question, but it came from my heart and became the path I pursued even though there were so many unknowns and financial risks. God reminded me of the verse, "We do not know what to do, but our eyes are upon you" (2 Chron. 20:12).

On July 7, I contacted Northeastern Seminary (which was only a thirty-minute drive from my house) and asked them about fall admission. The Admissions Coordinator told me they had an opening in the class, but the deadline for my application was July 15—eight days away! I had to fill out the application, write an autobiography, and find three people who would serve as references and be able to have their references on the admission's desk in one week. In addition, Houghton College had to get my transcript to their desk within that same timeframe. Having graduated from there thirty-seven years before, my records were in storage, but, "somehow," they were able to pull it off and had my transcript on the admission's desk before the deadline. On July 10, the Admissions Coordinator called to tell me they might be able to get me some financial aid and, on July 21, I received my formal acceptance into the fall semester.

Adding to my financial concerns, my computer—that I would need for writing multiple papers—quit working and I had to buy a new one. "Somehow" the money was available to purchase a new one. It was a huge blessing having a newer, faster, more reliable computer (which I never would have bought had my old one not quit) when I would be writing 70+ papers over the next two and a half years. It was just one of God's many blessings in the midst of so many unknowns and so much uncertainty. He brought to mind the verses, "In this world you will have trouble. But take heart! I have overcome the world" (John 16:33). "When you lie down, you will not be afraid; when you lie down, your sleep will be sweet" (Prov. 3:24).

My first night of seminary classes began Thursday, August 20. Although I was busy with house projects, leading a weekly church small group, a weekly community support group, and occasionally preaching, not having a full-time job on top of all that during my first semester of seminary was another one of God's blessings. After so many years of not writing research papers, it took much longer to write those first few papers, so it was a blessing to have the extra time to devote to reading, research, and writing.

On November 8th, our pastor resigned, on November 16th, the elders asked if I would be the interim pastor. On December 28th, the congregation voted "yes," and I officially started full-time ministry as interim pastor of our church on January 11, 2010. In August 2010, I was voted in as the permanent pastor, and I remained in that position until my retirement in November 2015.

Every time I think of those six months following the loss of my job, I shake my head in amazement. Seeing the abundance of God's blessing, love, and care throughout the entire process, and recognizing that the miraculous order and timing of events were so obviously orchestrated by the very hand and heart of God, filled my heart with profound gratitude—and still does today every time I pause and remember.

The ability to see God's hand of grace at work in our lives is something we need to practice and develop. It doesn't come naturally to us. As Elizabeth Dreyer says, "In a profound way, our intentionality is a key ingredient determining whether we notice God everywhere or only in church or only in suffering or nowhere."[8] We have to become intentional about watching, noticing, and truly seeing. Ruth Haley Barton says, "Learning to pay attention and knowing what to pay attention to is a key discipline for leaders [and I would add, for all of us] but one that rarely comes naturally to those of us who are barreling through life with our eyes fixed on a goal."[9] If we are to be intentional about seeing and responding in gratitude, we must slow down our lives and learn to listen, ponder, meditate, and hear God's voice. Barton continues, "The practice of 'turning aside to look' is a spiritual discipline that by its very nature sets us up for an encounter with God."[10]

Turning aside to look takes time, but we take time for many things in our lives like working, sleeping, eating, hobbies, entertainment, and nurturing our relationships. Why would we not take time to nurture the most important relationship we will ever have? In her well-known poem, Elizabeth Barrett Browning says,

> *Earth's crammed with heaven, and every common bush afire with God; but only he who sees, takes off his shoes— the rest sit around it and pluck blackberries.*[11]

Just as we must intentionally develop the art of "seeing" with the eyes of our hearts, we must also intentionally develop the ability to live with a grateful heart. Gratitude breeds gratitude. The more we nurture gratitude, the more we begin to see—all around us— that for which we can be grateful. Remember, we think about what we think about. What is it that our minds most often dwell upon? What do we think about in our quiet moments when we are not actively engaged in an activity? We will think about those things with which we most often fill our minds. Keeping a gratitude journal and daily writing one or more things for which we can be grateful can be one method of slowly turning our minds and hearts to a lifestyle of gratitude.

O Father, open our eyes that we might see, and as we see, may we truly be grateful—and may our gratitude transform our lives.

8

Waiting Patiently

Nearly everywhere I go, and everything I do involves waiting. I get in my car and wait for the slow driver in front of me. I wait at a red light or in the construction zone on the expressway. I go to a restaurant, wait for a table, wait for the server to take my order, wait for my food to arrive, and then, after I've eaten, wait for my check so I can pay and get on my way. I stop for a few groceries, carefully select what appears to be the shortest checkout line, then wait as I watch others—in lines I'd rejected—quickly and smoothly check out and head to their cars. On the way home, I make a dreaded stop at the Department of Motor Vehicles to document my change of address and endure the expected hour-long wait.

I'm thrilled when I see "Pre-TSA" printed on my plane ticket so I can rush through the security line only to arrive at the gate and discover my flight has been delayed—for hours.

I go to the physician's office, arrive on time, but have to wait to be seen. He then sends me to the lab where I have to wait some more. I make an appointment for a CT scan, arrive on time, but wait to be seen. I wait for a biopsy report. I wait to see if the radiation treatments will kill my cancer. When it appears to "work," I then wait for years to see if the cancer will recur. I lose my job and wait for a new one. I put my house on the market and wait for it to sell, and then wait while I try to find a new one. *Wait, wait, wait.*

What is the condition of my heart while I wait? My heart is usually tense, hurried, and driven. I'm busy. I have twelve items on my to-do-list and I want to get them all crossed off the list before the end of the day. Waiting slows me down and wastes my time. There is a feeling of uncertainty, helplessness, and a loss of control when I wait. And then, in the midst of all these frustrating "time-wasters," someone has the audacity to come alongside me and admonish me to "just be patient and wait." I don't have time to wait! Actually, what I really need is to get away from it all and take a vacation.

Unfortunately, I take my hurried heart along with me. I cram my vacation so full of activities that, when I come home, it takes me days to recover. With a fresh resolve to relax on my next week off, I schedule very little, saunter down to the beach, pull my lawn chair down by the edge of the water, and say to myself, "Okay, time to take a deep breath and unwind." But while my body is quietly sitting, my brain—still very much in "hurry" mode—begins to chide me, "Don't waste time, get up and do something, find something to see or do; after all, you can sit and do nothing when you get back home. You didn't travel all this distance and spend all this money just to come and sit, did you?" Or my brain shifts into hyper-planning mode and reminds me, "When you return home you'll have been gone for a week, so you'll have a lot to do. You'd better get it all organized now while you are sitting here wasting time so that you can hit the ground running as soon as you get home." My brain and heart silently, but persistently, chant in unison, "Rush, rush, hurry, hurry, be productive, don't waste time, fill every precious second accomplishing something of value."

Does anyone else struggle with this, or is it just me?

John Ortberg, the former Senior Pastor of Menlo Church in Menlo Park, CA, tells the story of when he once called and asked the late Dallas Willard, "What is the most important thing I need to do to be spiritually healthy?" After a long pause, Willard replied,

"You must ruthlessly eliminate hurry from your life." Another long pause. "Okay, I've written that one down," Ortberg replied a little impatiently. "That's a good one. Now what else is there?" Orberg explained, "I had many things to do, and this was a long-distance conversation, so I was anxious to cram as many units of spiritual wisdom into the least amount of time possible." Another long pause. Willard answered, "There is nothing else."[1]

Unfortunately, hurry isn't "out there" somewhere; it is deep within us and is damaging our hearts. Most of us *want* to "ruthlessly eliminate hurry from our lives," but we've tried to no avail. "Willing ourselves" to slow down does not work because our schedules are crammed full of appointments we "have" to keep; our daily "to-do lists," while impossible to complete, are filled with projects that just cannot wait—or so we tell ourselves. Although addressing our busyness will help—and is necessary—our "hurry problem" is much deeper, and the answer cannot be found by simply clearing our calendars or throwing away our to-do lists. Why are we so driven, and what is the solution? A heart that is irritated, frustrated, tense, and hurried in the midst of waiting is not the problem; it is only a symptom of something much deeper.

Can the Bible help us with this? Did the people described in the Bible have to do much waiting? What does the Bible say about waiting, and is it something to avoid or embrace? It only takes a cursory reading of the Bible to realize that waiting—lots of waiting—is a recurring theme from Genesis to Revelation. Noah obeyed God and built an ark; then he, his family, and the animals made it their home for a year. They waited while it rained, while the earth flooded, and while the water receded until the land was once again dry enough to walk on. A year was a long time to wait, living one day at a time, not knowing how long they would be confined in their floating house.

Despite Abram's and Sarai's advancing age, and despite Sarai's inability to conceive, God promised Abram (who was then 75 years old) that he would become the father of a great nation. Abram believed God and then waited, but Sarai didn't get pregnant. Hadn't God promised she would conceive and bear them a son? Was God going to fulfill His promise? Yes, but they would have to wait twenty-five years before Isaac was finally born, and Isaac was only one child, not a great nation.

At the age of forty, Isaac married Rebekah, who was also unable to conceive, and they also waited twenty-five years before Jacob was born. Ninety years had passed and now there were two—hardly a great nation. In His perfect timing, God fulfilled His promise to Abram (later to be named Abraham), but only after many years of waiting.

Joseph waited thirteen years (much of that time in prison) for the dream God gave him to come true. Moses waited forty years in the desert before God called him at the age of eighty to lead the children of Israel out of Egypt, where they had been held captive for four hundred years.

David waited at least fifteen years (most of that time fleeing for his life from an angry and jealous King Saul) from the time that Samuel anointed him to be the next king of Israel until he finally sat on the throne.

The Psalms are filled with exhortations to be still and to wait patiently. "We wait in hope for the Lord; he is our help and our shield" (Ps. 33:20). "Be still before the Lord and wait patiently for him; do not fret when men succeed in their ways, when they carry out their wicked schemes" (Ps. 37:7). "I wait for the Lord, my whole being waits, and in his word I put my hope. I wait for the Lord more than watchmen wait for the morning, more than watchmen wait for the morning. Israel, put your hope in the Lord, for with the LORD is unfailing love and with him is full redemption. He himself will redeem Israel from all their sins" (Ps. 130:5-8).

The Hebrew word for *waiting* is so multi-faceted that the translators used at least four different English words when translating that single word. Just within the book of Isaiah, that one Hebrew word is translated as "trust in," "wait for," "long for," and "hope in."

"In that day they will say, 'Surely this is our God; we *trusted in* him, and he saved us. This is the LORD, we *trusted in* him; let us rejoice and be glad in his salvation'" (Isa. 25:9, emphasis mine). This could have been translated, "We *waited* for Him and He saved us." The nature of godly waiting is *waiting in trust*. It is not blind, passive, wishful waiting. We are able to wait for God to act on our behalf because our trust is placed in His character—His goodness, faithfulness, love, and mercy. "Yes, LORD, walking in the way of your laws, we *wait for* you; your name and renown are the desire of our hearts" (Isa. 26:8, emphasis mine).

Knowledge of who He is—Almighty God, Creator, and Worker of Miracles—and what He has done in the past gives us the courage and strength to wait patiently for His perfect timing. "LORD, be gracious to us; we *long for* you. Be our strength every morning, our salvation in time of distress" (Isa. 33:2, emphasis mine). In the midst of our waiting, we long for God. We don't just long for God to act and "fix things" for us, but, because we hope and trust in Him, we long for a closer relationship and a greater intimacy with Him.

> *Why do you complain, Jacob? Why do you say, Israel, "My way is hidden from the LORD; my cause is disregarded by my God"? Do you not know? Have you not heard? The LORD is the everlasting God, the Creator of the ends of the earth. He will not grow tired or weary, and his understanding no one can fathom. He gives strength to the weary and increases the power*

of the weak. Even youths grow tired and weary, and young men stumble and fall; but those who hope in the LORD *will renew their strength. They will soar on wings like eagles; they will run and not grow weary, they will walk and not be faint.*

Isaiah 40:27-31

No matter how much we *feel* that God has abandoned us, forsaken us, lost touch with what we are enduring, or is unaware of our suffering or endless waiting, we must remind ourselves that because He is the everlasting God, the Creator of the universe, and the Knower of all things, we can be confident that our times of frustration and waiting are never hidden from Him. He is not apathetic or disinterested in our apparently hopeless situations. He knows eternity past to eternity future and is intimately involved in our lives. We can place our confident expectation in His care, and we can be assured that He will give us strength and courage so we don't grow weary or faint as we put one foot in front of the other. As we wait, and wait, and wait some more, we can rest assured we are not alone.

As mentioned above, "trust in," "wait for," "long for," and "hope in" all translate the same Hebrew word. While we wait for God, we trust in Him, long for Him, and hope in Him. They all help define how we wait. They are all woven together into one piece of fabric.

We place our trust and confidence in *God*, not in our circumstances. Our eyes are fixed on *God*, not the uncertainty, helplessness, and anxiety of waiting. Because our trust is in God and we long for Him and hope in Him, He can be our strength every morning, and we can rest in His love and care while we patiently wait.

Waiting should not be a frustrating, uncertain, boring, anxiety-producing, passive waste of time. We long for God, trust in Him, and place our hope in Him and, as we do, our strength will be renewed or, literally, our "strength will change" as though we're changing into a new set of clothes.[2] We will receive a totally new category, or quality, of strength that will see us through our time of waiting. We will no longer wait with our own inadequate, tired, and weary strength, but we will now wait with God's all-powerful strength.

In the face of adversity and suffering, the writer of the book of Lamentations says,

> *Yet this I call to mind and therefore I have hope: Because of the LORD's great love we are not consumed, for his compassions never fail. They are new every morning; great is your faithfulness. I say to myself, "The LORD is my portion; therefore I will wait for him." The LORD is good to those whose hope is in him, to the one who seeks him; it is good to wait quietly for the salvation of the LORD.*
>
> *Lamentations 3:21-26*

The Hebrew word that is translated "portion" means share, territory, or allotment.[3] What does the author mean when he says he is able to wait patiently because God is his portion? VanGemeren points to a verse in the book of Numbers—"The Lord said to Aaron, 'You will have no inheritance in their land, nor will you have any share among them; I am your share and your inheritance among the Israelites'" (Num. 18:20)—and explains that "in ancient Israel the priests enjoyed a privileged status of having the Lord as their 'share' and 'inheritance.'"[4] When the Promised Land was divided up, each tribe received a portion of that land. It was their share, their allotment. However, the priests and Levites did not receive a portion or allotment of land but, instead, were given God as their portion or inheritance.

In the same way, the writer of the book of Lamentations states that all he needs in his life is God. Because God is his portion or share or allotment, he needs nothing else. Because all his needs are met by God, he can patiently wait for God to act on his behalf.

The New Testament is also filled with multiple examples of those who waited. Even before Jesus is born, people are waiting. Elizabeth, Zachariah's wife, is advanced in years and has been unable to conceive. Through an angel, God promises Zachariah that his wife will bear him a son, but because Zechariah doubts the angel's promise, he is unable to speak. He waits nine months for his son to be born, unsure if he will ever speak again.

Mary, a virgin, is pregnant with Jesus and waiting for Him to be born, uncertain of what her life will be like as an unwed mother in this tiny village of Nazareth. Simeon and Anna have been waiting many years for the birth of the Messiah.

John the Baptist waits in prison, hoping Jesus—or someone—will rescue him. Jesus tells a poignant parable of a father who waits for the return of his wayward son. Mary and Martha wait four days for Jesus to arrive so He can heal their beloved brother, Lazarus. Jesus delays His trip *on purpose* and waits until Lazarus dies so He can raise him from the dead. After Jesus' death and resurrection, He tells His disciples to wait in Jerusalem until they receive the gift of the promised Holy Spirit.

God stops murderous Saul in his tracks and, in humility, Saul, whose name is changed to Paul, has to wait three days for Ananias to come and heal his blind eyes. Paul pleads and waits many years for God to remove his "thorn in the flesh." God does not answer his prayer but, instead, encourages Paul by telling him, "My grace is sufficient for you, for my power is made perfect in weakness" (2 Cor. 12:9).

The apostle James reminds us that, in the midst of our distress and suffering, our waiting must be seen in the context of the greater picture. "Be patient, then, brothers and sisters, until the Lord's coming. See how the farmer waits for the land to yield its valuable crop, patiently waiting for the autumn and spring rains. You too, be patient and stand firm, because the Lord's coming is near" (James 5:7-8).

The Greek word that is translated as "waiting" is not only "to watch for" something; it is also to "expect" that we will at some point receive it.[5] This definition parallels the Hebrew meaning of the word "wait." We wait in hope, and we wait in trust. James also reminds us that our waiting is not passive. The farmer works faithfully to care for his crops while he waits for the rains and the harvest. He knows they will not come tomorrow; he knows he must wait. He waits actively as he hoes and cultivates and weeds. He knows waiting is a natural and an expected component of farming, so he settles in, works hard, and waits.

Usually, we place *ourselves* at the center of our waiting. Even though we may not say it or even consciously think it, we feel, "Well, of course, I place myself at the center of my waiting! It is *me* who is waiting. God, look at *me* and help *me*. Why have you abandoned *me*?" But God and His purposes are much larger than *me*. The apostle Peter states,

> *But do not forget this one thing, dear friends: With the Lord a day is like a thousand years, and a thousand years are like a day. The Lord is not slow in keeping his promise, as some understand slowness. Instead he is patient with you, not wanting anyone to perish, but everyone to come to repentance ... So then, dear friends, since you are looking forward to this, make every effort to be found spotless, blameless and at peace with him.*
>
> *2 Peter 3:8-9, 14*

Jesus is coming again, and all will be made new. We long for His return, but we must wait for God's perfect timing. While we wait for His return, and wait during our times of suffering, anxiety, and uncertainty, we must remind ourselves that God lives outside of time and sees the big picture. He understands that even though it may seem to us like we are waiting a long time for Him to fulfill His promises and rescue us, during our waiting, He is eager for us to draw closer to Him so that we will more passionately trust Him, hope in Him, and long for Him.

EXPERIENCING WAITING

After living in our beloved farmhouse for over thirty-five years, we made the necessary repairs, placed it on the market, sold or gave away much of our stuff, packed up the rest, and moved an hour and a half away to be closer to our grandchildren. That is a one-sentence summary of what was to become a difficult lesson in learning how to patiently wait.

After discussing the process of selling our house with the first of three different realtors, on July 2, 2016, I wrote in my journal, "The ship has sailed from the harbor and we are on our way to Orchard Park, although I suspect there are many miles yet to travel and many curves in the road before this journey is complete."[6] Wow, that statement was certainly prophetic.

Our realtor listed our house on Monday, July 11th and, exactly two weeks later, July 25, we accepted an offer for $3000 more than the asking price. That was exciting and wonderful news, but that meant we must quickly find a new house. Despite viewing multiple houses in the Orchard Park area (some as far as 10 miles away), we found nothing that we felt we could call "home." Although I lost track of the exact count, we physically walked through thirty-five to forty houses after reviewing hundreds of prospective houses on internet sites. On August 2nd, while waiting for the realtor to arrive at one of the houses we were to see that day, we walked around the lot and, looking at each other, said, "This one has possibilities." Although it was clear it would need many repairs, the location was ideal. So, offering significantly less than the asking price, we placed an offer on the house the next day.

What we did not realize at the time was that the house was close to foreclosure and our low offer placed it in the category of a "short sale." This meant our offered amount fell short of the debts that had incurred against the property. In other words, if the bank were to accept our offer, they would receive less from us than what was still owed them by the previous owner. The daughter of the deceased owner quickly approved our offer; however, because it was a short sale, the bank also had to approve it. We heard nothing from the bank. A week later, our attorney seriously questioned the wisdom of waiting for the house. He told us, "These short sales can take a month—or in some cases, a year—to be approved. You don't have time to wait; you have to be out of your house soon." Unsure of what to do, on August 15th, I walked through the house with a professional house inspector and discovered even more needed repairs. Two days later, after a long talk with our attorney, we pulled the plug on our offer, decided we were back at the starting blocks in our search for a house, and resumed our hunt.

On August 23rd, I wrote in my journal, "For the first time in this house-hunting journey, I feel slightly "panicky" like we are on our own and we'll have nowhere to live."[7] The following day, I added, "Although I know it is not true, I certainly 'feel' alone, neglected, abandoned, and forsaken. I feel like God doesn't care; like if He did care, He would help. In the midst of all this, David's words in Psalm 27:13-14 are encouraging: 'I am still confident of this: I will see the goodness of the Lord in the land of the living. Wait for the Lord; be strong and take heart and wait for the Lord.' But, with David, I also cry out to God when he says, (v. 7) 'Hear my voice when I call, O Lord; be merciful to me and answer me.'"[8]

On August 24th, after looking at three more houses, none of which would meet our needs, we began to entertain the notion of finding an apartment to rent in the Orchard Park area. Temporary apartment living was certainly never included in our moving plan. Would we even be able to lease an apartment for less than a year? Would it take us a year to find a house? After multiple calls, God was gracious and we found an apartment complex in Orchard Park that would give us a three-month lease on a tiny 500 square-foot apartment. On August 26th, we drove to Orchard Park, signed a three-month lease with a move-in date for September 17th, signed a three-month lease for a storage unit and, feeling "spacey and twi-light-zonish," resubmitted our offer on the house we originally wanted and resolved to wait. On August 28th, I wrote in my journal, "This whole move has taken a toll on us! It will keep us young or kill us, one or the other. Thank you [directed in prayer to God] that You know the future and love us and extend mercy and grace to us and guide us into Your plan. It appears Your plan includes a three-month (or more!) detour into an apartment complex."[9] As was the case after the first offer, the bank again did not respond to us in any way following our second offer.

Moving Day, Saturday, September 17th, arrived. I awoke to dark, grey, ominous-looking clouds. After pausing to remind God that if our stuff got wet while loading the trucks in Henrietta or while unloading them in Orchard Park everything would be moldy by the time we pulled it out of the storage unit in three months (or longer), I jumped into my clothes and headed into the day. There was only a *very* brief, *very* light sprinkle of rain midway through the loading of our two seventeen-foot trucks despite the appearance that the clouds, at any moment, would open up and pour on us. Having loaded the last of our belongings, we slammed the doors shut and started down the road on our eighty-minute journey.

We had been driving less than fifteen minutes when the skies let loose and the rain came down in torrents. At points along the thruway, it was difficult to see the road through the pouring rain. The rain continued unabated for an hour. About five minutes before arriving at the storage unit, the rain began to lighten, slowed to a drizzle, and then stopped completely as we pulled up alongside our storage unit. We unloaded one full truck and half of the other at the storage unit and then drove the half-full truck over to the apartment where we unloaded the remainder of our worldly goods. After unloading everything, we served pizza to all those who had come to help. Just as we were eating our last few bites, it began to sprinkle again, so we cleaned up the pizza boxes and I returned the remaining rental truck.

The sprinkling of rain increased and, by the time I returned to the apartment, it was again pouring and it continued to pour throughout the rest of the night. What an unbelievable miracle and incredible gift from God in the midst of so much uncertainty and frustration related to our move.

On October 1st, after five weeks of waiting from when we submitted our second offer on the house, we finally heard that the bank had just now begun to deliberate. We also discovered it had taken a month for the realtors to even get our offer to the bank. (What?)

On October 5th, as a prayer to God, I wrote in my journal, "Having a plan, a sense of what will happen with the house, and a time frame in the journey toward closing, would help a lot. O Father, please guide us! Don't leave us alone! Don't leave us to wander this path on our own!"[10]

On October 7th, we received an email from the realtor stating, "Things are finally moving at the bank." We received no further communication until October 31st, when we received another email from the realtor stating, "Getting your house in the near future is looking pretty bleak." The bank was now asking the realtors to list the house on a foreclosure web site even though we had an offer on the table. They did not want to reject our offer, but neither did they want to accept it until they had explored all their options. We knew this possibly could add months to the process. I wrote in my journal, "Waiting is not easy, especially when there is no known end-point."[11]

Meanwhile, the apartment complex wanted us to pay another month's rent by the middle of November if we were going to stay past December 31st. What to do? We had no idea when, if ever, we would close on this house. On November 10th, I recorded in my journal, "I'm so deep down tired; not tired of waiting, but emotionally tired of not knowing what to do or where to turn—of feeling alone. Father, I declare that I am not alone, that You are right here with me and that You have a wonderful plan for our housing."[12] On November 11th, I called the realtor who informed me they hadn't heard anything. Not knowing what to do, we again began house-hunting. On the 14th, the realtor emailed me, "A bit of an email flurry on the house from the bankers, we'll see if anything comes of it!" On the 18th, the realtor called to say the bank had accepted our offer and, on the 21st, we received formal confirmation from the bank.

On November 26, I wrote in my journal, "I certainly am learning how to be patient and walk by faith and not by sight. I'm learning I can function, and live, one day at a time, without being in control and without being able to look into the probable future more than a few days."[13] After much back and forth and 'round and 'round, consistent with the bank's history thus far, we finally closed on the house December 19th. Because there was so much to do on the house, we decided to lease the apartment and storage unit for another month and did not move in until January 30, 2017.

In retrospect, four months was not a long time to wait, and we were blessed that events worked out as we had hoped and prayed; but, at the time, we had no idea what would happen, how long we would have to wait, whether we'd get the house at all, or if we should scratch the whole thing and begin our search all over again in the spring.

Being in the midst of waiting is quite different from looking back on the time of waiting, after the fact, from a place of "knowing the rest of the story." My experience was a good reminder that, if I want to truly understand the stories I read in the Bible and learn important lessons from those who have gone before me, I need to place myself in the story, in the middle of the waiting, without jumping ahead to the end of the story. Only then can I understand, learn, and appreciate their strength, courage, faith, and trust in the midst of their apparent helplessness, uncertainty, loss of control, and anxiety.

For many of us, we are still waiting for God to intervene on our behalf concerning a trial in our lives. Paul prayed for his "thorn in the flesh" to be removed, but God never removed it. I am still waiting for God to remove my "thorn in the flesh." (See Chapter 5: "Trusting God.") Some are unemployed and waiting for a new job. Others are waiting for enough money so they can purchase a house for their family. Some are waiting to get married or get pregnant. Others are waiting to become pain-free, cancer-free, or addiction-free. Others are waiting for their wayward child or their estranged spouse to come home. Some are waiting for _____; you fill in the blank.

None of us like to wait, but it's not about whether or not we finally receive that for which we wait but what happens to our hearts during our time of waiting.

Do you think Henri Nouwen was correct when he made the following statement? "For many people, waiting is a dry desert between where they are and where they want to go."[14] Does waiting draw us closer to God, or does it distance us from God? Pete Wilson states, "Spiritual transformation doesn't take place when we get what we want. It takes place while we're waiting. It is forged in us while we're waiting, hoping, and trusting, even though we have yet to receive what we long for. Spiritual transformation happens in the waiting room."[15] Matthew Anderson agrees and further states, "Waiting is a posture of the heart that establishes an atmosphere of trustful dependence regardless of the activities we are called to undertake."[16]

I am sure there are still lessons that have yet to fully develop in my mind and heart from my time of waiting, but there are others that are more immediately clear. First, waiting draws me into a more intimate, minute-by-minute relationship with God. As it did with the psalmists, I too find that, in the midst of waiting, I discover I need not fear voicing my true feelings of anxiety, frustration, and helplessness to God as I frequently and persistently call on God for wisdom, guidance, and help.

Second, I see God's power in the midst of my waiting. My faith and trust in God strengthens as I see His hand move on my behalf in many ways, reassuring me of His continual, loving presence and care.

Third, my character grows while I wait. My motives, priorities, values, passions, and desires slowly transform to conform to those of the heart of God.

Fourth, waiting trains me to live in the moment, not in the future, and to give up control of my future and place it in God's hands. I know nothing of what the future holds—even though I vigorously strive to control it—but God sees the future very clearly.

Fifth, waiting melts my controlling, independent, self-sufficient tendencies and draws me to humility and dependence on God.

Sixth, as I wait, my trust in, hope in, and longing for God grows. As my trust, hope, and longing grow, I find that I begin to focus less on my desires and what I want God to do for me and more on what *God's* desires are for me.

Learning these lessons and truly living in their reality will not just benefit me during the difficult times of waiting in my life; but, as my tense, anxious, driven heart begins to heal, it will also find peace and relax during the ordinary and routine waiting I encounter in my everyday life.

My prayer is that "waiting patiently" will become a lifestyle and that David's testimony will become mine. During a low point in his life, he wrote, "I waited patiently for the Lord; he turned to me and heard my cry. He lifted me out of the slimy pit, out of the mud and mire; he set my feet on a rock and gave me a firm place to stand. He put a new song in my mouth, a hymn of praise to our God. Many will see and fear and put their trust in the Lord" (Ps. 40:1-3). As David patiently waited, God heard his cries for mercy and lifted him out of his despair, and David responded with a heart of grateful praise. David's experience with God did not benefit just David but benefitted many who, because of observing David's life, placed their faith and trust in God.

9

Encouraging Each Other

Sadly, we live in a world where we are more likely to focus on each other's "opportunities for improvement" and offer correction rather than focus on each other's strengths and offer affirmation and encouragement. Jess Lair observes that, "Praise is like sunlight to the warm human spirit; we cannot flower and grow without it. And yet, while most of us are only too ready to apply to others the cold wind of criticism, we are somehow reluctant to give our fellow the warm sunshine of praise."[1] Dallas Willard agrees and asks, "Could we successfully negotiate personal relations without letting people know that we disapprove of them and find them to be in the wrong? Condemnation—giving it and receiving it—is such a large part of *normal* human existence that we may not even be able to imagine or think what life would be like without it."[2] One math teacher, however, not only imagined what life *could be* like but created a warm caring environment that, as a result, demonstrated what life *was* like and how it dramatically impacted one of his students.

I had a great feeling of relief when I began to understand that a youngster needs more than just subject matter. I know mathematics well, and I teach it well. I used to think that was all I needed to do. Now I teach children, not math. I accept the fact that I can only

> *succeed partially with some of them. When I don't*
> *have to know all the answers, I seem to have more*
> *answers than when I tried to be the expert. The young-*
> *ster who really made me understand this was Eddie.*
> *I asked him one day why he thought he was doing so*
> *much better than last year. He gave meaning to my*
> *whole new orientation. "It's because I like myself now*
> *when I'm with you," he said.*[3]

Imagine living in an environment where we could depend on consistent encouragement rather than criticism, and imagine the impact this would have on our children, our grandchildren, our marriage, our workplace, or our church fellowship. It sounds refreshing, but how would we create, or even describe, such an environment? Are terms like *flattering, applauding, admiring, praising, affirming,* and *complimenting* just different words to describe what it means to encourage each other? And why do we even need each other's encouragement? Since the Holy Spirit encourages us—"[the church] enjoyed a time of peace. It was strengthened; and encouraged by the Holy Spirit, it grew in numbers, living in the fear of the Lord" (Acts 9:31)—and Scripture encourages us—"For everything that was written in the past was written to teach us, so that through endurance and the encouragement of the Scriptures we might have hope" (Rom. 15:4), shouldn't that be sufficient?

Although we may think it is a sign of weakness when we feel starved for encouragement, biblical writers make it very clear that encouraging each other is vital to our physical, emotional, and spiritual health. If this is such an essential skill, why do most of us struggle with doing it well? Could the dearth of volunteers, the lack of ministry involvement, the high burn-out rate, the ever-en-larging numbers of those drifting from the faith, or the high resig-nation rate of our church pastors be related to poor or nonexistent encouragement skills within the church family? What does God, as revealed through the writers of the Bible, have in mind when He speaks of encouragement and how to effectively offer it to others?

The New Testament Greek word that is translated as "encourage" is a rich word with many facets and nuances that cannot be captured through the use of but one English word. Therefore, depending on the context and the author's intended meaning, the same Greek word has been variously translated into English as urge, encourage, beg, plead, comfort, console, appeal, exhort, or request.[4] Likewise, in the Old Testament, most of the Hebrew words that are translated "encouraged" are also variously translated into English as strong, strengthen, found strength, took courage, or urged.

As we study the Bible and reflect on the breadth of its meaning, we quickly discover that encouraging each other is a multifaceted, profound, and essential responsibility that must transcend a hasty pat on the shoulder with a perfunctory, "Good job!" or "Hang in there; you can make it!" if we are to thrive, flourish, mature, and grow as God intended.

As we review the above list of methods we might use to encourage each other, we can quickly recognize that we rarely use only one method during any given encounter. For example, while ministering to a grieving individual, we may unconsciously blend together comfort, strengthening, exhortation, and urging without giving any thought to which element of encouragement we are utilizing. However, for purposes of clarity, I want to separately explore four of these methods: strengthening, exhortation, comfort, and consolation.

ENCOURAGING EACH OTHER THROUGH STRENGTHENING

God spoke to Moses, a wise and beloved leader, and used him in powerful ways to lead the nation of Israel out of slavery. He parted the Red Sea so they could walk across on dry ground, provided fresh drinking water from a rock, established a system for worshiping God, and led the people through forty years of desert wanderings. When, at the age of one hundred and twenty, he died. "The Israelites grieved for Moses in the plains of Moab thirty days, until the time of weeping and mourning was over" (Deut. 34:8). "After the death of Moses the servant of the Lord, the Lord said to Joshua son of Nun, Moses' aid: Moses my servant is dead" (Josh. 1:1-2a,). Why did God state the obvious? Joshua knew Moses was dead; he had just spent a month mourning for him. It was time for Joshua to set his eyes on the future because the nation of Israel needed a new leader and God was appointing him to this role.

I suspect Joshua was terrified, discouraged, and anxious, and felt weak, uncertain, and inadequate to replace Moses, but God repeatedly reassured, encouraged, and strengthened him for his new role. God said, "Be strong and courageous" (1:6), "Be strong and very courageous" (1:7), "Be strong and courageous" (1:9). Sometimes we need to hear a truth more than once before it begins to trickle from our heads and sink deeply into our hearts.

The Hebrew word that is here translated as "strong," is the same word translated as "encourage" in multiple other verses in the Old Testament.[5] God said, "No one will be able to stand up against you all the days of your life. As I was with Moses, so I will be with you; I will never leave you nor forsake you" (1:5). How did God's encouragement strengthen Joshua? First, God strengthened (encouraged) him by reminding him of the past. As Joshua heard the phrase, "As I was with Moses," it must have instantly transported him back to forty-plus years of experiences when God's presence and power (demonstrated through Moses) were clearly evident.

Second, God strengthened (encouraged) Joshua by giving him hope for the future. As He had empowered Moses, God's power would now flow through Joshua. God said, "So I will be with you" (1:5), and "I will give you every place where you set your foot, as I promised Moses" (1:3).

Third, God strengthened (encouraged) Joshua by challenging and inspiring him to remain spiritually healthy because only then would his endeavors be successful. "Do not let this Book of the Law depart from your mouth; meditate on it day and night, so that you may be careful to do everything written in it. Then you will be prosperous and successful" (1:8).[6]

Fourth, God strengthened (encouraged) Joshua with the promise of His continuous presence. "Have I not commanded you? Be strong and courageous. Do not be terrified; do not be discouraged, for the Lord your God will be with you wherever you go" (1:9).

How did God's strengthening (encouragement) mobilize Joshua in the midst of his fear, discouragement, anxiety and feelings of inadequacy?

> *So Joshua ordered the officers of the people: "Go through the camp and tell the people, 'Get your supplies ready. Three days from now you will cross the Jordan here to go in and take possession of the land the Lord your God is giving you for your own.'"*
>
> *Joshua 1:10-11*

Just as God encouraged and strengthened Joshua, we can also encourage and strengthen each other. When some are faced with a task for which they feel fearful, anxious, or inadequate, we can challenge them to remain spiritually healthy, and we can remind, inspire, and encourage them with how God has worked in the past, how He will always be with them, and how His promises can give them hope for the future. God's words, spoken through our lips, can give them courage to not lose heart and can motivate, energize, strengthen, and embolden them to accomplish great things for God and for the building of His kingdom.

Encouraging Each Other through Exhortation

If we are to effectively encourage, there are times when we must "preach" to each other. Although we might perceive these times of exhortation (when we challenge, urge, admonish or powerfully persuade each other to action) as harsh or intrusive, if shared gently, lovingly, and kindly, they can help open our eyes to our "blind spots," can encourage us to make some needed changes, and can help us see the bigger picture of our lives in the context of all of eternity.

John the Baptist preached to and baptized the people who came to hear him. "And with many other words John *exhorted* (encouraged) the people and preached the good news to them" (Luke 3:18, emphasis and parenthesis added). John's exhortations (see 3:7-14) were not easy to hear. He warned them of the coming judgment and called them to a repentance that leads to lifestyle changes. John explained that they could evaluate the authenticity of their repentance by observing the way in which they treated the poor and the degree to which kindness dominated their interactions with others. Why would Luke refer to these difficult teachings as encouragement? Why were they not viewed as offensive, judgmental, and convicting? John's preaching occurred in the context of, and was intimately associated with, the hope-filled and exciting good news of the arrival of the long-awaited Messiah. John is an excellent model for when we "preach" to each other. If our exhortations are to encourage, they must not only point to areas of needed change, but they must also open the eyes of our hearts to see the big picture of how our motives, values, and priorities affect not only our lives today but all of eternity.

All exhortations need not leave us feeling "preached to." In a spirit of exhortation, Jesus encouraged His disciples (and us) when He said, "I have told you these things, so that in me you may have peace. In this world you will have trouble. But take heart! I have overcome the world" (John 16:33).

The apostle Paul encouraged those who were grieving in the church in Thessalonica (along with those of us who are also grieving now) when he reminded them that, after the dead in Christ rise, "we who are still alive and are left will be caught up together with them in the clouds to meet the Lord in the air. And so we will be with the Lord forever. Therefore encourage each other with these words" (1 Thess. 4:17-18). We, too, can profoundly encourage each other when we "preach" the very words of God as found in the pages of Scripture.

The book you now hold in your hands is the result of words of exhortation (encouragement) that were "preached" to me on two different occasions. In the middle of the 2013 Spring Semester of my third year in seminary, after handing me a graded paper at the end of class, my professor told me, "You should write a book." Although it was only a five-word sentence, it spoke paragraphs to me and had a profound impact on my heart. Those five words not only encouraged me at that moment but planted a seed in my heart that slowly began to grow.

Five years later, while sharing lunch with a close friend, he asked, "So ... when are you going to start writing your book?" A few weeks later, I sat down and began to write. Most of us considerably underestimate the power of an encouraging word, but a word of exhortation, offered in love, can change our lives.

Encouraging Each Other through Comfort

We are a people who love comfort. We love the comfort of our old, nearly worn out, warm sweater or baggy sweat pants. We will search near and far and pay extra money for a pair of comfortable shoes. We wrap ourselves in the comfort of our fluffy, quilted blanket—appropriately termed a comforter. When tired or stressed, we reach for "comfort food." We adjust the thermostat in our house to a comfortable temperature. We prefer to remain in our "comfort zone"—that place that is predictable, relaxed, safe, and stress-free.

However, this is not the comfort of which the apostle Paul refers when he writes that God is "the God of all comfort, who comforts us in all our troubles" (2 Cor. 1:3b-4a). When God comes alongside us in the midst of our trials, His intent is to encourage us, not to make us "feel good." The Greek word that is here translated as "comfort" is the same word that is translated "encourage" or "encouragement" in other passages.

> *Praise be to the God and Father of our Lord Jesus Christ, the Father of compassion and the God of all comfort (encouragement), who comforts (encourages) us in all our troubles, so that we can comfort (encourage) those in any trouble with the comfort (encouragement) we ourselves have received from God. For just as the sufferings of Christ flow over into our lives, so also through Christ our comfort (encouragement) overflows. If we are distressed, it is for your comfort (encouragement) and salvation; if we are comforted (encouraged), it is for your comfort (encouragement), which produces in you patient endurance of the same sufferings we suffer. And our hope for you is firm, because we know that just as you*

> *share in our sufferings, so also you share in our com-*
> *fort (encouragement). (parentheses added)*
> *2 Corinthians 1:3-7*

God's comfort—and subsequently our comfort toward others—encourages and strengthens us in the midst of our pain, distress, or grief. Although the translators could have used the word "encourage" in this passage, using "comfort" expands and clarifies the direction that, on occasion, our encouragement must take. Sympathy or empathy alone may or may not truly comfort others but can be a component of "encouraging comfort."

Our perspective changes when we view comforting as encouragement, not just as sympathy or empathy. When we begin to understand this difference, we do not merely ask ourselves, "How can I comfort those who grieve," but we ask ourselves, "How can I encourage them with my comfort." Some of the more common statements we may voice such as, "I'm so sorry for your loss," or "I have a bit of a sense of what you may be going through because I also lost a child," may comfort but may or may not encourage. What can we say that might, with sympathy, empathy, and tenderness, also infuse them with strength and courage to "stay the course" and not lose heart? How can we comfort and encourage them without taking biblical truths out of context or using them in a clichéd or trite manner? How can we avoid having them feel disrespected—like we think they should just "look on the bright side" or "snap out of their grief?" We need to remember that although well-chosen words can be life-giving, the gift of our presence and physical touch (when appropriate) can, at times, be more encouraging and comforting than spoken words. However, at some point, we need to audibly offer something but, when we do, what should it be? Knowing just the right thing to say can be difficult because that which may comfort and encourage one person may be painful to another.

Only a few months after my son Ben was killed in a car accident, an acquaintance approached me and asked, "When I teach my driver ed. students, may I have your permission to use Ben's death as an example of why it is so important for them to wear their seat belts?" (Although we never had to remind Ben to fasten his seat belt when he drove with us, for some reason that night, while in the back seat of his friend's car, he chose not to use it. Since there is a high likelihood that, had he been buckled up, he would have survived, his negligence in this matter was, and still is, a deep source of pain.) I responded graciously and consented to his request. Although this encounter was painful, I am convinced this individual was attempting to comfort and encourage me—and, in a way, he probably did. He perhaps reasoned that it would help bring meaning and purpose to Ben's death if, as a result of his teaching and sharing Ben's tragic story, other students might take seatbelt usage to heart and, should they also be involved in an accident, their lives be saved.

Unfortunately, because knowing what to say is so often difficult and we fear hurting those who grieve, for many of us, our default is to say nothing—which also can be hurtful. Because we so desperately need each other's comfort and encouragement, this is just another reason—among many—why we need to maintain a close, conversational relationship with God so we can hear the Holy Spirit's "still small voice" during these times of uncertainty and confusion. We must spend time in prayer, plead for Holy Spirit guidance, carefully ponder how we might encouragingly comfort those in deep distress and grief, and then trust that we will hear the words the Holy Spirit would have us offer.

Encouraging Each Other through Consolation

I never tire of the Christmas story and the many interesting, inspiring, and thought-provoking interactions that Luke records in his gospel. He writes of the interactions between the angel and Zachariah, Zachariah and Elizabeth, Gabriel and Mary, Mary and Elizabeth, the angels and the shepherds, the shepherds and Mary, Joseph, and Jesus, and of the interactions between the new family and Simeon and the new family and Anna when Joseph and Mary consecrate Jesus in the temple.

The Holy Spirit revealed to Simeon that, before he died, he would see the Messiah for whom he had waited so many years. "Now there was a man in Jerusalem called Simeon, who was righteous and devout. He was waiting for the *consolation* (encouragement) of Israel, and the Holy Spirit was upon him" (Luke 2:25, emphasis and parenthesis added). The Greek word that is here translated as "consolation," is the same word that is elsewhere translated as "encouragement." The long-expected One, Jesus the Messiah, was coming to console Israel. Why wasn't Simeon waiting for the "encouragement of Israel" or the "comfort of Israel"? Perhaps, the translators used "consolation" rather than "encouragement" or "comfort" to emphasize the facet of encouragement that includes not only comfort, solace, and sympathy, but also relief.[7] Jesus came to comfort, encourage, and strengthen His people, but He also came to bring them relief. He came to restore them, redeem them, and rescue them from spiritual slavery. Jesus did not come just to sympathize and empathize with them; He came to do something about it. We too, can encourage others, not just with our words but also with our actions—tangibly offering relief for their burdens.

A few years ago, on one of our bi-yearly trips to Palmetto, Florida, to visit my mother, we decided to fly into Orlando rather than Tampa because the flight and rental car were substantially cheaper. Anticipating the two and one-half hour drive across the state, after obtaining our rental car, I was eager to get going. I briefly inspected the car then jumped in. I noticed that the tire warning light was on but, since the tires looked fine, I reasoned one tire was a bit low on air and it wouldn't matter.

I drove the one hundred and thirty miles to our condo on Anna Maria Island without incident, pulled into the garage, unloaded, and settled in. Although it was now "obvious" that I was justified in ignoring the tire warning light, when convenient, I still planned to top off the air pressure in the underinflated tire.

The next morning, without even checking the tires, we jumped into the car and headed down to Palmetto to visit my mother. A mile or two from the condo, while still on Gulf Drive, I began to hear a loud, "thump, thump, thump, thump" coming from the right rear tire. This was accompanied by the tell-tale sensation that we were rhythmically driving over a series of bumps in the road. I groaned as I pulled over to the side of the road. Sure enough; our right rear tire was completely flat. Although changing a tire was not what I wanted to do on that hot and humid morning, I got out of the car and opened the trunk to retrieve the jack and spare tire. I lifted the floor panel to encounter a completely empty tire cavity.

"You can't be serious!" I grumbled. (Okay, it was a trace more than a grumble.) I called the rental company to complain, but they politely advised me that most car manufactures no longer include a spare tire as standard equipment. They reassured me they would be happy to repair the tire if I arranged to have the car towed to the nearest rental office fifteen miles away. I can't remember exactly what I said to them, but I'm pretty sure my response was polite, kind, and demonstrated gratitude for all their considerable help (don't I wish!).

While I was pondering what to do, "out of nowhere," a smiling gentleman walked up to me and asked if he could help. With a pained smile, I pointed to the very flat tire.

He looked at it and commented, "Hmmm, looks like you have a flat tire."

I just smiled at him but said to myself, "Do you think?"

He then said, "Let me look." Literally, within ninety seconds, he found a screw deeply embedded within the tread. "Hold on just a minute," he said and then disappeared as quickly as he had appeared. After fifteen minutes had passed, I wasn't sure what to think, but then a truck pulled up behind me. He got out with his tire-puncture repair kit and, within minutes, extracted the screw, inserted a special adhesive covered plug, cut off the extra rubber tail, hooked up his portable tire inflator, and partially inflated my tire. He then told me to follow him and drove another mile down the road to a filling station where he inserted his own quarter into the air pump. He filled my tire to the proper pressure, and thirty to forty-five minutes from when he first appeared, he drove away in his truck.

Did he encourage me? Yes! But, even better, he consoled me. He comforted, sympathized, empathized, and exhorted me, but he also brought me relief. He didn't just leave me in my misery and broken-down state; he restored me and my car's flat tire. He freed me from the bondage of a car sitting helplessly along the side of the road.

ENCOURAGING EACH OTHER THROUGH OUR EXAMPLE

Although we usually think of verbal, face-to-face, one-on-one contact as the best way to encourage each other, we can be profoundly impacted by observing or reading about the lives of others and how they were able to find strength and courage in the midst of their frustrations, challenges, hardships, and suffering.

Jerry Sittser encouraged me when I read how, in one dark night in the midst of a horrific auto accident, he tragically lost his mother, wife, and four-year-old daughter.[8] I identified with his unspeakable pain and sorrow and marveled at how he was able to survive those first few days, weeks, and months by taking one step at a time. Through his writing, I observed his journey of grief and how his dependence on God's grace and mercy kept him sane and allowed him to return to work and to settle into a new routine at home. I observed how he was able to keep the relationship with his surviving children intact, despite his profound sadness. Reading about his life encouraged me also to draw strength and comfort from God's grace and not lose heart in the midst of my grief. His story challenged me that, even in the midst of my tears, I too, could take heart, stay the course, and continue to know and experience the love and goodness of God.

Brennan Manning encouraged me when, through his books, I observed the depth of his humility, openness, and honesty. His final book, published a couple of years before his passing into glory, was especially frank about his struggle with alcohol.[9] Most well-known, prominent individuals try to cover up their faults and minimize the issues with which they struggle. However, Manning, who spoke to thousands of people in numerous retreats, wrote multiple books, and was well known and loved, laid out his life for all to see. He challenged me that, despite my pride, my desire to please people, and my inclination toward perfectionism, my health, the health of those around me, and the building of God's kingdom are all enhanced when I, too, am humble, open, and honest.

Peter Scazzero's writings encouraged me to look below the surface of my life and to evaluate my emotional health.[10] He helped me see that it was impossible for me to be spiritually healthy if I was not also emotionally healthy. Sharing his own journey of emotional health challenged me to follow his example.

Instead of slowing down after retirement, a married couple in our church ratcheted it up and, following the guidance of the Holy Spirit, developed, lead, and—well into their eighties—sustained an effective ministry among the international students in the local community. Their example is an encouragement to me that, no matter how old I become, I can continue to seek opportunities to minister to those around me.

Watching a friend valiantly and uncomplainingly battle cancer until it destroyed his physical body, encouraged me to raise my eyes above the steady stream of nuisances in my life and reminded me to fix my eyes on that which is unseen and eternal, not on that which is seen and temporary (2 Cor. 4:18).

If we open our eyes to truly "see" those around us and take the time to pause and notice, we could all list multiple examples of how others, without saying a word to us, are regularly encouraging, challenging, exhorting, urging, comforting, and strengthening us by the way in which they faithfully live out their daily lives.

Encouraging Ourselves

Although it may be challenging for some of us, we cannot fruitfully encourage others if we cannot encourage ourselves. There is a poignant story in 1 Samuel 30 where, in the midst of a tragedy, David admirably modeled his ability to do this. At one point in his life, while he was running from murderous King Saul, he and his six hundred men who followed and supported him (along with their wives and children) lived in the city of Ziklag. One day while David and his men were away on a mission, the Amalekites invaded the Negev, attacked Ziklag, burned it to the ground, and took everyone captive. When David and his men returned, they discovered that their dwellings and everything they owned had been reduced to ashes and that not one family member was to be found, "So David and his men wept aloud until they had no strength left to weep" (1 Sam. 30:4). "David was greatly distressed because the men were talking of stoning him; each one was bitter in spirit because of his sons and daughters" (30:6a).

How would I have responded had I been in David's sandals? I suspect I would have felt profound guilt that I was unable to protect our families after my men had trusted me and had abandoned their "routine lives" to follow me. I would have been confused, disappointed, and angry that God had not protected our wives and children while my soldiers and I were away from home. I would have wrestled with anxiety, fear, and indecision. Perhaps David also felt all these emotions; but, instead of sinking into despair, he "found strength in the Lord his God" (30:6b) (or, as stated in the English Standard Version, "But David strengthened himself in the Lord his God."). The Hebrew word that is here translated as "found strength" or "strengthened himself" is the same word translated in other passages as "encouraged."[11]

David encouraged and strengthened himself in the midst of this apparently hopeless circumstance by drawing upon God's encouragement, strength, comfort, and his previously cultivated intimacy with God. From that strength, he was then able to rally his men, devise a plan and, with their help, rescue their families.

How was David able to pause, strengthen himself, encourage his men, and then move forward? Perhaps one reason was the quality of David's "self-talk." As a result of his past experiences, he knew how to effectively "preach" to himself. He often talked to his own inner soul, reminded himself to worship God, and rehearsed all that he knew to be true about the love and goodness of God.

After exhorting himself to worship, he penned the words, "Praise the Lord, O my soul: all my inmost being, praise his holy name. Praise the Lord, O my soul and forget not all his benefits" (Ps. 103:1-2). Other psalmists also "preached" to and encouraged themselves: "Why are you downcast O my soul? Why so disturbed within me? Put our hope in God, for I will yet praise him, my Savior and my God" (42:5). "Be at rest once more, O my soul, for the Lord has been good to you" (116:7).

What about me? Sometimes I cringe at my self-talk. Sometimes my self-talk is wise and my theology is solid, but my *heart* struggles to believe and accept it. It is curious that effectively encouraging myself to affirm the love and goodness of God following a series of "trivial" problems can sometimes be more demanding than encouraging myself following a major crisis. Although each trivial issue is a minor frustration, when stacked up one on top of the other, their accumulated weight can, unconsciously but gradually, erode my ability to acknowledge that God is good to me.

For example, just recently, the underground pipe that carries my sump pump water to the storm drain by the road plugged up and was deemed by the experts to be irreparable. I had an emergency pipe placed to carry the water out onto the lawn until the warmer weather arrived when a full replacement pipe could be installed.

The caulk around the bathroom tub and up the sides of the tub-surround was old, moldy, and ugly, so I spent hours scraping it all out and properly cleaning the joint in preparation for the new caulk. I shopped for a quality caulk that would not mold, would stay white, and was flexible and crack-proof so that I would not need to re-caulk for years to come. After a few days, the new caulk cracked and I had to re-caulk every joint.

Soon thereafter, I had just gotten started working on a project in my woodworking shop when my dust collector accidently sucked up a large piece of paper that promptly got stuck in the impeller. So, instead of completing my project, I used the remainder of my shop time pulling the machine apart to retrieve the errant paper.

Then, I walked down to the basement where I discovered that, for no apparent reason, a random copper hot water pipe joint was dripping. Then ... well, I could go on and on. Can you relate?

During times like these, God regularly brings me back to Psalm 46:10, where God, through the psalmist, exhorts me to "Be still, and know that I am God; I will be exalted among the nations, I will be exalted in the earth." God is God; always has been, always will be. God knows what transpires during every minute of my life and comes alongside me and urges me to pause to strengthen and encourage myself to press on without frustration or discouragement. He urges me to recall to memory all that which I know to be true and to focus my eyes not on my present circumstances but on the bigger picture of the greatness and goodness of God.

Mutual Encouragement

At the risk of stating the obvious, encouragement must be mutual or reciprocal, and is therefore a responsibility for all of us—not just for pastors, leaders, or those with the spiritual gift of encouragement (Rom. 12:8). In his letter to the church in Rome, the apostle Paul reassures them that he has, on multiple occasions, planned to visit them, and his hope is that God will soon enable him to see them so that he can strengthen them, and that they "may be mutually encouraged by each other's faith" (1:12).

Humanly speaking, Paul's faith was fathoms deeper than the young, growing faith of the Christians in Rome. We would anticipate that Paul's trip would clearly encourage the church but perhaps fail to assume the reverse. However, Paul affirms that the purpose of his journey is for *mutual* strengthening and encouragement. He expects to be built up and encouraged by them just as they will be by him. He receives from them, and they receive from him. The level of spiritual maturity or experience does not dictate the direction to which, or from which, encouragement flows. We all have something to offer each other—from the youngest to the oldest, the least spiritually mature to the most spiritually mature, the least formally educated to the most formally educated—irrespective of IQ points, dollars in the bank, prefixes before our name, physical attractiveness, location or size of our house, or the make or age of our car.

Mutual encouragement is just that—you encourage me and I encourage you. I don't look down on you or look down on myself; we look across at each other and, on equal footing, encourage each other.

True mutual encouragement can only transpire in an environment of shared openness and honestly and can never thrive in an environment of competition or jealousy. Whether I regularly gather with a small group of individuals or interact one-on-one with a friend, I must examine myself and ask God for a humble heart and a sensitivity to see their needs and struggles while opening my life—with all my needs and struggles—to them.

Random Concluding Thoughts

First, sometimes we carefully need to plan our words of encouragement, not just share what spontaneously pops into our mind in the moment. The author of the book of Hebrews gives us a glimpse into the intentionality and urgency with which we are to encourage each other. "Let us *consider* how we may *spur* one another on toward love and good deeds. Let us not give up meeting together, as some are in the habit of doing, but let us encourage one another—and all the more as you see the Day approaching" (Heb. 10:24-25, emphasis added). Because the day of Christ's return is approaching, the writer prompts us to encourage each other to love, do good deeds, and regularly meet together.

For many of us, the word "consider" may denote giving something a bit of thought. If someone approaches us with a request for help, we might respond with "Okay, I'll consider it," which means we briefly weigh the pros and cons and quickly come to a decision. However, the Greek word that is here translated as "consider" is a much stronger word. It means to "[focus] one's complete attention on something," or to contemplate and ponder something to the point of understanding.[12] When we "consider," we think about what we will do or say in enough depth to clearly "see" what God would have us do. We reflect and thoughtfully ponder. We compare ideas, mull them over in our minds, and contemplate if they will truly encourage others to pursue that to which God is calling them. We continue this reflection until we feel confident that our encouraging words or actions will "[build them] up according to their needs" (Eph. 4:29b).

The Greek word that is here translated as "spur" means to provoke, irritate, pester,[13] exasperate,[14] or sharpen.[15] Although this word generally carries a negative connotation, it is used here in a positive sense. In some situations, the best encouragement may be when someone "harasses" us into doing that which we know is best, even when it takes us out of our "comfort zone." However, we must be acutely aware that if provoking, pestering, irritating, exasperating, or sharpening is to be a positive experience in someone's life, it must be done with love and kindness after carefully reflecting on ("considering") how that encouragement will benefit them and how it will benefit the building of God's kingdom.

Second, sometimes, when we compliment or affirm others, our comments (such as: "you did a great job") are so generic that, although they may temporarily make them feel good, they often do not truly strengthen or encourage them.

I was a pastor of a small community church for several years and that experience opened my eyes to how we might better encourage our pastors after they preach on Sunday morning. When we say something like, "I really identified with that story you told because I've been in that same situation myself," it encourages them. They realize that the stories they tell have an impact on the hearts of their listeners. Or when we say, "I've never heard it stated like that before; it helped me more clearly see how much God loves me," it encourages them that the time they spend trying to say things in fresh ways really opens up our eyes. Or if we say, "I really struggle with trying to live that out in my daily life, so what you said helps me see how I need to depend more on God for His help and how I need to start spending more time alone with Him," it encourages them that people's lives are being impacted by what the Holy Spirit has placed in their heart to share on Sunday morning.

None of these statements *predominantly* compliment or affirm them but can deeply encourage them to stay the course and not lose heart in the midst of pastoral ministry that at times can feel thankless.

Third, sometimes encouraging others involves humility. Pride is perhaps *the* most common reason we do not truly encourage each other. Sometimes, to affirm and encourage others in their areas of gifting means I must admit—to myself and to them—that I do not excel in that area. This is especially difficult when the area of gifting I am affirming in someone else is an area in which I personally want to excel. Pointing out their strengths can be humbling. To affirm and encourage someone who has shared something that speaks to my heart about a needed change in my life is to admit that I struggle in that area and need help. Admitting my struggles to you can be humbling because, after all—we erroneously reason—considering my age and the number of years I have been a Christian, I should, by now, already know "everything" and victoriously be living it out in my daily life.

As is the case with everything else in our spiritual journey, encouraging each other cannot be accomplished in a vacuum. Everything we think, do, and say is interrelated and interconnected. Therefore, if we are to learn to encourage ourselves and others well, a growing, healthy, intimate relationship with God must be foundational to everything we say and do.

10

Standing Firm

T he title of this book, *Seeing the Unseen: Learning to See with the Eyes of our Hearts*, describes a skill that is important for understanding every topic discussed, but perhaps it is most critical for understanding and living out the message of this chapter. Although we may believe in the existence of something that is unseen, because it is not visible, we are inclined to ignore it or to minimize its significance and thereby seriously downplay the impact it has on our lives. The world of microorganisms is one unseen world that, for many centuries, wreaked havoc on our lives because we did not believe any such world existed.

For all you American history aficionados, the dates of April 12, 1861-May 9, 1865, mean but one thing: The American Civil War. The standard answer given for the number of soldiers who perished in the war is usually six hundred and twenty thousand, but some say that number may be as high as eight hundred and fifty thousand.[1] How did so many soldiers die? Well, they got shot, of course, right? No, two-thirds of them, that is two out of every three soldiers who died in the war, did *not* die as a direct result of the injuries they sustained on the battlefield.[2] *Two thirds.* So how did they die? How did more than four hundred thousand soldiers die in that horrific war? Who, or what killed them?

An unseen world.

A world they could not see, and that most people did not believe existed, killed them. What unseen world? The world of bacteria and viruses—better known as germs. Diseases such as typhus, typhoid, dysentery, smallpox, and yellow fever killed many of those four hundred thousand, and thousands died from infected wounds or infected amputations.[3] If only they had known about thoroughly cleansing wounds or quarantining the sick, many thousands of lives could have been saved. Why didn't they know this?

Five years *before* the Civil War began, an English nurse, Florence Nightingale, became famous for her care of wounded soldiers in the Crimean War (October 5, 1853-March 30, 1856).[4] The death rate of soldiers in the hospitals where she worked was impressively low due to her insistence on overall cleanliness, the careful cleaning of wounds, and her fresh air policies.[5] Hadn't those caring for the wounded in the Civil War heard about this? Perhaps no one had come over to America to tell them, or perhaps they had heard but just rolled their eyes and said, "Whatever."

Although Girolamo Fracastoro proposed the germ theory as early as 1546[6] and Marcus von Plenciz expanded upon those views in 1762, for the most part those beliefs were held in distain.[7] "Only wacko scientists with nothing better to do with their time believe in that nonsense!" One hundred years later, during the Civil War (1860-1864), a French biologist by the name of Louis Pasteur conducted research linking germs with disease that finally began to change scientific thinking.[8]

Perhaps those in America had not yet heard about the significance of Pasteur's research or they had heard but did not believe it. "We can't see those germs, so how can they be real? An unseen world teeming with invisible little bugs that are killing us? Not likely!" However, in just one four-year long war, this very real and very dangerous unseen world of little bugs killed over four hundred thousand soldiers while medical personnel were either ignorant of this world or knew about it but brushed it aside as irrelevant. If only they had known; if only someone had told them in a way they could have understood and applied it to their protocols for caring for the sick and wounded, they could have made choices that would have saved thousands of lives. Tragic? Yes, mournfully tragic.

Today, in 2020, one hundred and fifty-five years after the end of the American Civil War, we are once again fighting for our lives in what President Donald Trump and US Army generals are calling a war against an unseen enemy.[9] For the first time since the Civil War, New York City's Central Park has been converted into a field hospital to help care for the multiple thousands who are ill and dying—sickened by the unseen world of a new virus called COVID-19.

Unlike during the time of the Civil War, today there is no one who questions the existence of this unseen virus; however, because we cannot see it, we do not know which surfaces are contaminated or who is carrying the virus—until they become ill or request testing. The strategies we use to fight a war against an unseen enemy like COVID-19 are vastly different from the strategies we use to fight a war against a visible enemy and, because the enemy is hidden from our view, many more lives will perish before this grim pandemic is defeated.

We are also fighting for our lives in another war waged in the unseen world—the spiritual world—that is just as real but vastly *more* significant than the world of microbes. Unfortunately, because the spiritual world cannot be seen, many people are either ignorant of it or do not believe in it, declare it absurd, roll their eyes, ignore it, or brush it aside with distain and contempt, convinced it is irrelevant to their daily lives. Some may say, "An unseen spiritual world that impacts my life in any meaningful way? Not likely!" or, "Only superstitious wacko religious fanatics with nothing better to do with their time believe in that nonsense!"

However, ignoring this unseen spiritual world is much more dangerous and results in immensely more serious consequences than ignoring the unseen world of germs. Ignoring the microbial world impacts our lives for the few short years we live here on earth, but ignoring the spiritual world impacts our lives for eternity. Although this is not new information for most people, many continue to brush it all aside as inconsequential to how they live their lives. They may say, "I've got things to do, I'm busy; when things settle down, I'll give more thought to God and eternity. Besides, all that talk about being in a constant spiritual war with an invisible enemy makes me tired."

Our spiritual wholeness depends upon our awareness of, and our ability to see and stand against, the attacks of our spiritual enemy. Since the devil's strategies are numerous, if we are to stand firm, we must be mindful of the many creative schemes he utilizes to wound, deaden, or distance our hearts from God.

C. S. Lewis' book *The Screwtape Letters*[10] is a humorous but very insightful and often poignant reminder of the diverse means the devil employs to wage war against our souls. The book is a collection of letters written by Screwtape (the devil) and sent to a budding tempter—his nephew, Wormwood. In one letter, Screwtape's advice to Wormwood is, "Keep his mind on the inner life ...You must bring him to a condition in which he can practice self-examination for an hour without discovering any of those facts about himself which are perfectly clear to anyone who has ever lived in the same house with him or worked in the same office."[11] In another letter, Screwtape muses, "It is funny how mortals always picture us as putting things into their minds: in reality our best work is done by keeping things out."[12] Other pointers include, "Keep rubbing the wounds of the day a little sorer even while he is on his knees,"[13] or "All extremes, except extreme devotion to the Enemy are to be encouraged."[14] (Screwtape's Enemy is, of course, God.) We may have to pause for a few minutes and ponder these morsels of guidance to Wormwood to fully recognize how subtle but effective they are in keeping us from maintaining a healthy relationship with God, ourselves, and others.

The apostle Paul cautions us that "Satan ... masquerades as an angel of light" (2 Cor. 11:14). We wear costumes and masks to transform our outward appearance when we attend a masquerade party, but that costume does nothing to change our inner nature. I could wear a very realistic bear costume, lumber around the room, stand on my hind legs and menacingly growl or viciously swipe my clawed paw at one of the other guests. But, inside that costume, I am still Bob.

This is the meaning of the Greek word that is here translated as "masquerades."[15] Satan masquerades, or outwardly disguises himself, as an angel from God, but within that costume of light there is nothing but darkness—darkness bent on slandering, deceiving, and spiritually crippling us.

We may be already heavily involved in various worthy ministries when the desperate need for a volunteer within our church family is made known. The task is something we could do well and, although agreeing to help would spread us thin, we say "yes" because we are convinced God wants us to assist in such a valuable ministry. We rarely ask ourselves if it is really God who wants us to get involved or if it is the masquerader of light who is urging us to do yet one more thing to minimize our effectiveness in our other ministries and to unbalance other important responsibilities. Or, God may *want* us to assist in the ministry, but the masquerader of light twists the truth a bit and chides us with, "don't forget your top priority is responsibility to your family," so we say "no." Being informed of this strategy, staying alert, praying, and maintaining an intimate relationship with God will aid us in discerning between God's light and Satan's costume of light.

The apostle Peter warns us that the devil is not always subtle in his attacks but sometimes "prowls around like a roaring lion looking for someone to devour" (1 Peter 5:8b). This lion is not slinking around quietly; he is roaring. His intention is to weaken our integrity, destroy our wholeness, and draw us away from the heart of God by attempting to intimidate and frighten us. However, as we make ourselves aware of the devil's schemes, we need to be careful that we do not begin to fear the devil and "see him everywhere" and assign to him power that he does not have. The apostle John reminds us that "the one who is in you is greater than the one who is in the world" (1 John 4:4).

In this unseen spiritual war in which we are engaged, it is essential we be aware that it is not only the devil who attempts to draw us away from God's heart, but we must also contend with the allure of the world and the desires of our sinful nature. When we say "yes" to Jesus' gift of salvation and commit to follow Him, the power of sin is broken, and we are then no longer slaves to the devil, the ways of the world, or the desires of our sinful nature. Unfortunately, however, in our humanness, we still experience the pull toward all that which distances us from intimacy with God and must therefore learn how to stand firm against that dangerous undertow that is ever ready to suck us underwater and out to sea.

Although some may disagree, it matters not to me if the dangerous undertow originates from the devil, the world, or the desires of our sinful nature—they all draw us away from unity with the Father, Jesus, and the Holy Spirit. Our response to the undertow therefore must be the same: we must stand firm against it.

If I am relaxing on the beach where multiple people are strolling around in various degrees of undress and a woman catches my eye, I must resist the temptation to take a second look. I do not need to engage in a theological discussion with myself to determine whether the devil is tempting me, the desires of my sinful nature are drawing my eyes to "look," or if my twenty-first-century American culture is encouraging me to take what is not mine and enjoy this tempo-rary pleasure—without caring how it will injure my heart. It makes no difference which of the three is trying to wound me, because no matter what name I give it, my response should be the same—I must stand firm against it, look away, and redirect my eyes to the pelicans skimming the water or the dolphins surfacing between the wave crests out in the gulf.

How can we consistently stand firm against our unseen enemies in the spiritual world that threaten to destroy our intimacy with God? The apostle Peter tells us to control ourselves, be alert, be vig-ilant (not drowsy, absent-minded, or preoccupied), maintain a clear mind, resist him (refuse to take the bait), stand firm in the faith, and draw strength from knowing we are not alone in our struggle (1 Peter 5:8-9).[16] James instructs us that if we submit to God and resist the devil's deception, intimidation, and fear-mongering, he will flee from us. (James 4:7).

The apostle Paul also gives us guidance on how we can success-fully stand firm.

> *Finally, be strong in the Lord and in his mighty power.*
> *Put on the full armor of God so that you can take your*
> *stand against the devil's schemes. For our struggle is*
> *not against flesh and blood, but against the rulers,*
> *against the authorities, against the powers of this dark*
> *world and against the spiritual forces of evil in the*
> *heavenly realms. Therefore put on the full armor of*
> *God, so that when the day of evil comes, you may be*
> *able to stand your ground, and after you have done*
> *everything, to stand. Stand firm then with the belt*
> *of truth buckled around your waist, with the breast-*
> *plate of righteousness in place, and with your feet*

*fitted with the readiness that comes from the gospel
of peace. In addition to all this, take up the shield of
faith, with which you can extinguish all the flaming
arrows of the evil one. Take the helmet of salvation
and the sword of the Spirit, which is the word of God.
And pray in the Spirit on all occasions with all kinds
of prayers and requests. With this in mind, be alert
and always keep on praying for all the saints.*

Ephesians 6:10-18

Standing firm against all that would spiritually harm us requires strength, but we need God's strength because ours will never suffice. God's mighty power—the same power that raised Jesus from the dead (Eph. 1:18-21)—is available to each one of us who believe and receive Jesus' gift of salvation. Even though this incredible, divine power is sufficient to meet our every need, we also have a part to play, so the apostle Paul uses a Roman soldier as a metaphor to help us understand how we can protect ourselves against our invisible spiritual enemy.

Paul mentions six essential pieces of armor and cautions us that, if we are to stand firm, we must avail ourselves of the entire armor package. In this spiritual war, Paul tells us not to advance against or attack the enemy but to "take your stand" (6:11), "stand your ground" (6:13), and "stand firm" (6:14). Our mission is to firmly stand our ground without retreating or falling down while we defend ourselves against the devil's varied schemes. Although this analogy can be confusing, if we are to protect ourselves from joining the rapidly growing list of spiritual casualties, we must understand and learn how to apply this insightful metaphor.

BELT OF TRUTH

Although the NIV translators perhaps wished to avoid using an antiquated and therefore little understood phrase, in so doing, they significantly diluted the richness of this aspect of preparing for spiritual battle. It is therefore helpful to read the NASB translators' rendering of this phrase which states, "Stand firm therefore, having girded your loins with truth." "Okay," we might respond, "perhaps that translation is more accurate, but what are our loins, and what does it mean to gird them?"

The long flowing robes or tunics worn in the first century made running, working, or fighting problematic. As a result, before fishermen, farmers, or other laborers began to work or before soldiers put on their armor, they girded up their loins. (Although "loins" specifically meant the lower back muscles, when used, the term usually referred more generally to the entire lower torso.) This meant they would take their long tunic, pull it up to their upper thighs, pass the ends of the fabric between their legs, and then bring the ends around their waist and tie them in a knot.[17] This allowed them to run, work, or fight more easily unencumbered by the folds of clothing that otherwise would hang down around their legs. For added security against the tunic becoming unfastened in battle, soldiers buckled a girdle ("belt") around the gathered fabric. In addition to securing the tunic, the girdle also provided some degree of protection and support for the lower torso and was frequently a place from which to hang the scabbard for their sword. Once the tunic was girded, the rest of the armor could be secured in place.

Spiritually, the first step to prepare for battle is to "gird up our spiritual loins" (that is, remove all that would hinder us and thwart our ability to fight effectively) with truth. Knowing and living the truth is essential, or error and half-truths will encumber our ability to stand firm against the attacks of our spiritual enemies.

Unfortunately, for the most part, our twenty-first century "politically correct" American culture no longer believes in "ultimate truth." Our culture declares "truth" to be relative. It insists that "truth" for me may not be "truth" for you, and vice versa. It declares it is fine for me to believe whatever I like as long as I don't foist my beliefs on you. God's word, however, tells us differently.

The God who created the universe and sustains it with His power is the source of all truth. Jesus declared, "I am the way and the truth and the life. No one comes to the Father except through me" (John 14:6). Jesus also declared, "If you hold to my teaching, you are really my disciples. Then you will know the truth, and the truth will set you free" (John 8:31-32). While praying on behalf of His disciples, Jesus asked God to, "Sanctify them by the truth; your word is truth" (John 17:17b). For soldiers, tucking their tunic into their girdle freed their legs for battle. For Christ-followers, knowing the truth and holding firmly to the truth by "wrapping ourselves in it" frees us to stand firm against the enemy's fabrications and deceptions.

Truth is not just something we believe but something we live. "Wrapping ourselves in truth" frees us to discern between good and evil, to say "no" to evil, and to fight against it. The apostle John tells us, "If we claim to have fellowship with him yet walk in the darkness, we lie and do not live by the truth" (1 John 1:6). If we know the truth, we will obey Jesus' teachings and say no to the evil promptings of the devil.

Truth is not only something we believe and live, but also something we speak. The truth draws us to moral integrity, truthfulness, and honesty.

Without ultimate truth, the other pieces of armor are pointless. Without ultimate truth, God's righteousness, peace, and salvation are open to question. Without ultimate truth, our faith is in vain. Without ultimate truth, God's word is of little value. When we wrap ourselves in God's truth by believing, living, and speaking the truth, we are ready to secure the other pieces of armor and take our stand against the enemy.

In his endeavor to deceive us, we usually assume the devil will dilute the truth by tempting us to incorporate the latest culturally accepted beliefs. However, sometimes he is perfectly content to leave the truth intact. When a small group of Christ-followers gather to study the Bible, he is delighted when, instead of lovingly discussing it, we argue about what it means and our opinionated comments wound each other, dilute the richness of God's truths, and glorify logic at the expense of mystery.

Breastplate of Righteousness

The breastplate was a critical piece of armor because it protected the upper body—most importantly the heart and lungs—from injury. A penetrating wound to the soldier's heart would most certainly prove fatal.

Spiritually, protecting and maintaining a healthy heart is also a matter of life and death. The writer of the book of Proverbs urges us, "Above all else, guard your heart, for it is the wellspring of life" (Prov. 4:23).

We guard our hearts not just by keeping the wrong stuff out but also by keeping the right stuff in. We guard our hearts when we fill them with what we know to be true about God, His goodness, and His love; we keep it fresh by regularly recalling it to memory (See Chapter 1: "Remembering God's Acts of Grace"). We also guard our hearts when we deny entrance to evil thoughts. Whether good or evil, everything that gains access to our hearts is a seed that implants itself and grows. Nothing we see, hear, or touch is neutral. The *good* will grow, flourish, and nurture our hearts; the *evil* will also grow and flourish, but it will destroy our hearts. We must therefore, guard and protect our hearts with our spiritual breastplate.

The guard and protector of our spiritual hearts is righteousness. Righteousness is God's perfect moral standard for living.[18] Since God's standards are impossible to attain, we create our own standards and attempt to live by them even though they are unacceptable to God. However, the apostle Paul tells us that "There is no one righteous, not even one; there is no one who understands, no one who seeks God. All have turned away, they have together become worthless; there is no one who does good, not even one" (Rom. 3:11-12). In God's eyes, "all our righteous deeds are like a polluted garment" (Isa. 64:6, ESV).

Our only recourse is to accept *God's* righteousness which He freely and gladly offers us. God declares us righteous when we place our faith in Jesus. "God made him [Jesus] who had no sin to be sin for us, so that in him we might become the righteousness of God" (2 Cor. 5:21). When we believe and receive Jesus, God gives us a spiritual breastplate—righteousness—to guard and protect our hearts, but we must accept it and strap it on. That means living in that righteousness by obeying God's commands while remembering that God calls us to *be* righteous people, not just to *do* righteous deeds.

Dallas Willard tells us that our "goal is not to be people who do loving things but to become the kind of people who naturally, joyfully, and easily love."[19]

So often, it is not the "big-sin temptations" that trip us up but the daily, seemingly insignificant, temptations against which we struggle to stand firm. This is especially true in our attempt to consistently demonstrate respect, love, patience, gentleness, kindness, and forgiveness to those we love the most—our own families. Willard awakens us to reality when he says, "Most families would be healthier and happier if their members treated one another with the respect they would give to a perfect stranger."[20]

SANDALS OF PEACE

Roman soldiers wore thick-soled sandals studded with hobnails that laced up around their ankles. These "sandal-boots" protected their feet, and the nails provided good traction, especially during hand-to-hand combat. A soldier could not fight effectively without healthy feet.

Spiritually, if we are to stand our ground against the attacks of our unseen enemy, we also need reliable and protective footgear. According to Paul's metaphor, that which will give our feet protection, traction, and a firm footing is the good news of peace. Although there is disagreement among theologians as to whether this peace refers to our personal peace or the sharing of the gospel of peace with others, to my mind, these two should be viewed as one continuous whole.

There are three aspects to this peace. First, we obtain peace with God when we, through faith, accept Jesus' gift of salvation. "Therefore, since we have been made right in God's sight by faith, we have peace with God because of what Jesus Christ our Lord has done for us" (Rom. 5:1, NLT). Because of Jesus' sacrificial death on the cross, our relationship with God (which was broken when sin entered the world) has been reestablished.

Second, our peace with God leads to peace within our hearts. "Ruthless trust"[21] in the goodness, love, and continual presence of God will bring peace to our hearts and will repel anxiety that threatens our ability to stand firm against the attacks of the enemy. Jesus says, "Peace I leave with you; my peace I give you. I do not give to you as the world gives. Do not let your hearts be troubled and do not be afraid" (John 14:27). The apostle Paul tells us, "And the peace of God, which transcends all understanding, will guard your hearts and your minds in Christ Jesus" (Phil. 4:7). Paul uses military terminology to personify peace as a sentry marching back and forth across the door of our hearts—protecting them against anxiety invasion.

While typing this chapter, right in mid-sentence, the thought suddenly popped into my mind that several weeks ago, I had mailed tax forms to my accountant but hadn't heard anything back from him. When that thought popped into my mind, I stopped writing and immediately called him, only to confirm my suspicion that he never received them. Where were they? Were they lost, or had someone stolen them? With all my social security numbers, pension account numbers, and life insurance policy numbers contained in that envelope, did I now have to be concerned with potential identity theft?

Although anxiety wanted to flood my heart in that moment, how could I let that happen when I was right in the middle of writing about it?! Instead, I listened to another voice, "Bob, stand firm against the enemy of your soul who is trying to defeat you and tense you up with anxiety." Amazingly, I allowed God's peace to be a sentry marching across the door of my heart, I gave the problem to God, and I declared to Him along with David that "Those who know your name will trust in you, for you, Lord, have never forsaken those who seek you" (Ps. 9:10).

Unfortunately, these "little things" happen to us on a regular basis. Each time they occur, we can choose to trust or worry. When we stand in our sandals of peace, we can stand firm against the devil's temptations and not allow him to defeat us with tenseness and anxiety. (In case you were wondering, my accountant eventually received my tax forms thirty-six days after I mailed them!)

Once we obtain peace with God and peace with ourselves, the natural progression is to share the good news of that peace with others. Sharing the gospel of peace with others is, in itself, an act of war against the enemy because, when we share, others will experience the joy and freedom of peace with God and peace with themselves. "How beautiful on the mountains are the feet of those who bring good news, who proclaim peace, who bring good tidings, who proclaim salvation, who say to Zion, 'Your God reigns!'" (Isa. 52:7).

SHIELD OF FAITH

The fourth piece of God's armor is the shield. Although predominately a defensive weapon, it was also used offensively to push against the enemy. The shield was not fixed to the body as was the breastplate but was held up with one arm and could be moved in any direction to screen the body from a javelin, sword, or arrow. Sometimes enemies would affix a flammable substance to the arrow tip and then set it on fire before releasing the arrow. Due to excessive weight, the first-century shields were rarely constructed of metal but, instead, were usually fashioned of wood covered first with canvas or linen, then with animal skins. The skins, when thoroughly soaked with water before battle, would help extinguish the flaming arrows.

Spiritually, the shield that will intercept and quench the unseen enemy's blazing arrows is faith. The Greek word that is here translated into English as "faith" can refer to believing, trusting, or having confidence in God, it can refer to the collection of our Christian beliefs, or it can refer to living a faithful or trustworthy life.[22] Although we do not know for sure which of these facets of faith Paul had in mind when he commanded us to take up the shield of faith, it really makes little difference because they are all interrelated and cannot properly be separated one from another. In the minds of the New Testament authors, true belief in God was inseparable from faithful living. Faithfulness (the same Greek word that is translated as "faith") is one of the elements of the Fruit of the Spirit (Gal. 5:22). Paul's ministry was to call people "to the obedience that comes from faith" (Rom. 1:5). Luke records that "a large number of priests became obedient to the faith" (Acts 6:7). Each facet of the collection of our Christian beliefs contributes to our belief, trust, and confidence in God as we stand our ground against the enemy who is bent on destroying our hearts.

When we believe God's promises, have confidence in His goodness and love, and fully trust God with our lives—past, present, and future—our minds and hearts will be fully fixed on God, and our faith will be a shield against anything the devil hurls at us. We need to recognize that major crises in our lives, which the devil can use to spiritually attack us, are, for the most part, in the minority. Yes, there will be times when a coworker may attempt to seduce us into an adulterous affair. A sudden tragedy in the family may persuade us to "throw in the towel," give up on God, and quit following Him. A Stage Five cancer diagnosis may kindle within us a rage against God. A close friend may hurt us so deeply that we resolve never to forgive. However, these life-changing crises are less common than the ordinary, daily, annoying, "tiny darts" that life throws at us. Although we usually ignore, or are oblivious to, our daily annoyances, the devil can use them to slowly but steadily defeat us.

A tiny dart may be when we feel offended and, without questioning our feelings, allow indignation to rise up within us? Where is our shield when that indignation progresses to frustration, then to a slow-burning anger, then to a coldness in our relationship which persists for weeks, or maybe years? Where is our shield when envy creeps into our heart after our friend buys a brand-new car while the only thing keeping our car together is the rust molecules? Where is our shield when that envy turns to bitterness, then resentment, then becomes a tiny but very real wedge in our relationship? Where is our shield when our spouse says something that annoys us but, instead of letting it go, we reply with a cutting rejoinder? Where is our shield when we don't even *want* to use our shield because, in an odd sort of way, it feels good to reciprocate? These are just a few examples of the types of "flaming arrows" we experience most days of our lives that we must learn to extinguish with our shield of faith/faithfulness.

HELMET OF SALVATION

The bronze helmet worn by Roman soldiers was a vital piece of armor because, without it, their head—the control center of their body—was prominently exposed and subject to sustaining life-threatening blunt trauma, deep lacerations, or penetrating injuries. To advance into battle without a helmet was folly.

Paul tells us that if we are to stand firm in battle against the evil one, salvation will be the helmet that will protect our minds. Clear thinking is of paramount importance if we are to successfully defend our ground against the devil who tells us lies and half-truths in an attempt to confuse us, cause us to question our long-held beliefs, or discourage us by flashing images of past failures before our minds.

What does it mean to use salvation as a helmet? Isn't salvation something God gave us in the past when we said "yes" to Jesus' gift of salvation and believed and received Him (John 1:12)? If we are "saved," then isn't salvation now a part of our DNA and defines our status before God? If this is true—and it is!—then why is Paul telling us to put on our salvation like a soldier puts on a helmet? How do we put on something that already defines who we are?

First, and foremost, we must clearly understand that because of God's grace, salvation is free. There is nothing—zero—we can do to earn it. "For it is by grace you have been saved, through faith—and this not from yourselves, it is the gift of God—not by works, so that no one can boast" (Eph. 2:8-9). Through faith, we receive God's gift and are then born into His family. However, just like physical infants grow from helplessness to maturity, Peter tells us that spiritually we too must "grow up in [our] salvation" (1 Pet. 2:2) and Paul tells us that our salvation is something we "work out" (Phil. 2:12).

If a nurtured human baby does not develop and grow, we rightly become apprehensive. So, too, nurtured spiritual infants born into God's family will grow. Accepting God's gift of salvation births us into His family, but we still need to grow and mature. Nurturing new spiritual life is not "working" *for* our salvation; it is merely evidence that salvation has occurred. To repeat, just like nurtured human infants grow, so, too, nurtured spiritual infants grow. If we do not grow, it should cause us concern.

God's salvation is not something we set aside on a dusty shelf in our minds and then chalk it up to a necessary but completed task that will provide us with an admission certificate to heaven when we die but then go back to living unchanged lives. We live our salvation, grow in our salvation and, during battle with the unseen enemy, protect our thinking with salvation.

Commonly, the devil attempts to discourage us by questioning our salvation and our standing before God by reminding us of our past failures, the hurtful words we voiced in anger, our fears and anxieties, and all the times we doubted God's love and goodness. It is not uncommon for a random event to suddenly flash before my eyes. The picture may be of a time when I spoke hurtfully sarcastic words to one of my boys when they were young. Above the picture flashes the words, "Terrible Father!" Or, the image may be of a time when I was rude and disrespectful to my wife, and the words, "Poor excuse for a husband!" blaze across the picture. Or my mind may flashback to the time when, thinking it was the leading of the Holy Spirit, I planned a large-scale, two-week sports camp as an outreach for our church that we had to cancel because only five children registered. At the top of the picture, written in flashing neon lights, is "Failure!" I view the "video clips," wince, and wish I could go back and re-do those events, but I can't. Nevertheless, the devil attempts to use these flashbacks to impugn my worth as a child of God, discourage me, and cause me to give up the fight.

Our helmet of salvation, however, will protect our minds so that we promptly and precisely remember that God's salvation and our standing before Him originate in grace, and His grace is unaltered by our failures. God's salvation saves us from the penalty of sin, the power of sin, and from the power of the enemy. We *can* stand firm against him, not because of how great, strong, wise, or righteous we are, but because *God's* greatness, strength, wisdom, and righteousness flow through us. We can fight with confidence because our minds are razor sharp and crystal clear on the truth of God's salvation—freely given to us.

SWORD OF THE SPIRIT

As is the shield, the sword is also both an offensive and a defensive weapon. It can be used to wound the enemy, or it can be used to avoid injury by deflecting the opponent's sword. The sword mentioned here by Paul was not the large, broad sword but the shorter sword (like a large knife or dagger) that every soldier carried in his belt and was the sword most often used during hand-to-hand combat.[23]

Spiritually, our sword is God's Word. Jesus beautifully modeled for us the power and effectiveness of this sword when He stood firm against the devil's attacks in the wilderness by quoting from the Old Testament book of Deuteronomy (read Matt. 4:1-11). Jesus was able to successfully fight the devil with God's words because He had read them, studied them, meditated on them, and memorized them.

If we are to use the Holy Spirit-inspired words of God as a defense against the devil, we too must read them, study them, meditate on them, and memorize them or know where to find them in the Bible so we can look them up and use them as a defense against the devil's attacks. In prayer, the psalmist voiced, "I have hidden your word in my heart that I might not sin against you" (Ps. 119:11).

We can utilize God's Word to fight the devil during every one of his attacks. Go back and review each of the previous chapters in this book. What scriptures can we declare that will help us stand firm so we do not forget what God has done for us in the past? How can understanding the scriptural metaphors for God or metaphors for the church help us resist the devil? What does God's word say about times of intense grief when we are tempted to lose hope? How can we neutralize anxiety and trust God when life seems to be falling down all around us? How can we fight against the devil's lies that spending time alone with God is a waste of time? How can we stand our ground against the temptation to be ungrateful for God's blessings because He doesn't "fix" the crises in our lives that matter most to us? How can we take our stand against the devil when he whispers that our long times of waiting for God to answer are evidences that God is not present, does not care, or both? How can we combat and repel the snide allegations that our church family does not care about us or value us? We stand our ground against all these attacks with God's Word.

Not only can we use God's Word to defend ourselves, but we can use it as an offensive weapon. We can help push back the darkness of the devil's domain when we share God's Word with others who have not yet heard or have heard but have not yet understood. God's Word will work in their hearts and minds and draw them to respond to Jesus' gift of salvation and thereby deal a wounding blow "against the powers of this dark world and against the spiritual forces of evil in the heavenly realms" (Eph. 6:12).

PRAYER

Although some scholars argue that Paul includes prayer as the seventh weapon, since he does not assign an armor metaphor to it as he does the other six, it is more likely that bathing our entire lives in prayer is what Paul had in mind. Theologian Clement of Alexandria (AD 150-215) described prayer as "keeping company with God."[24] Constant communication with God is the foundation upon which we must build our entire lives. It is in this context of "keeping company with God" that we remain alert and are thereby able to quickly detect the advances of the enemy. We pray in the power of God, and when "We do not know what we ought to pray for ... the Spirit himself intercedes for us with groans that words cannot express. And he who searches our hearts knows the mind of the Spirit, because the Spirit intercedes for the saints in accordance with God's will" (Rom. 8:26a-27).

Paul offers Epaphras as a model for us: "Epaphras ... is always wrestling in prayer for you, that you may stand firm in all the will of God, mature and fully assured" (Col. 4:12). Let us join Epaphras and wrestle in prayer for each other because, as Frank Laubach reminds us, "Nobody but God knows how often prayers have changed the course of history."[25]

Questions for Reflection and Discussion

Introduction

1. What does it mean to see with the eyes of our hearts?
2. Discuss 2 Corinthians 4:18.
3. Read the story in 2 Kings 6:8-17. Put yourself in the story and take a moment to ponder what you would have thought and how you would have felt. How did the servant's perspective dramatically change during this crisis when he could finally see the reality of the unseen world?
4. In the midst of our trials, how might our perspective change if the eyes of our hearts could see God at work beneath the surface of our problems?

Chapter 1: Remembering God's Acts of Grace

1. Describe a time when God's grace was abundantly evident in your life.
2. In what ways did remembering, and then relating that story to others, cause your confidence in God to grow?
3. Read Deuteronomy 4:9. What are some of the reasons we so easily forget God's acts of grace?
4. Read Psalm 77:1-15. What was it that transformed the psalmist's heart from lament to praise?

5. What are some concrete things we can do to help us remember God's acts of grace so that they do not slip or fade from our hearts?

Chapter 2: Enriching Our Understanding of God through Metaphors

1. Can you relate with Elihu, David, Isaiah, Paul, and others when they declare that God is beyond our understanding?
2. Do the biblical metaphors for God enrich your understanding of God or merely confuse you?
3. What has been your favorite, or most commonly used, metaphor for God? After reading this chapter, do some of the other metaphors now hold a richer meaning for you?
4. Name and discuss some of the other metaphors for God that are not mentioned in this chapter.
5. Read Romans 11:33-36. What bubbles up in your heart as you read these verses?

Chapter 3: Enriching Our Understanding of the Church through Metaphors

1. Describe your involvement and experience in the local church. Has it been predominately positive or negative?
2. Which of the eight biblical metaphors that are mentioned in the chapter best help you understand the nature of the church? Explain your answer.
3. Read 1 Corinthians 12:12-26. Although this may be a very familiar portion of Scripture to many of us, read it as though you are reading it for the first time. What implications do these concepts have for you, your family, the church, and how you relate to each other?

4. Discuss the analogies of planting an acorn in a terrarium or placing a sundial in the shade. Was there a time in your life when the church did not benefit from your gifts and talents?

5. Spend some time discussing the seven metaphors that were only briefly mentioned. How does each metaphor enrich our understanding of the church?

Chapter 4: Grieving with Hope

1. Describe a time when you experienced grief.

2. In the midst of your grief, what evidences of God's love, care, and compassion did you see?

3. Read 1 Thessalonians 4:13. What does it mean to grieve with hope?

4. How might biblical hope differ from our common use of the word "hope"?

5. Read John 11:1-37. What can we learn from this story about grief, hope, and trust in God?

Chapter 5: Trusting God

1. Describe a time in your life when you felt abandoned by God.

2. What did you learn about God, and what did you learn about yourself as a result of that experience?

3. Is any of that knowledge useful to you now in your present trials?

4. The psalmist says, "Be still and know that I am God" (Ps. 46:10). While we are still, what is it about God that we are to know?

5. Read Habakkuk 3:17-19. In our journey of trust, could we ever get to the place where we could agree with Habakkuk?

Chapter 6: Spending Time Alone with God

1. Describe your experiences in your time alone with God.
2. Have you given much thought to whether or not God enjoys your times with Him?
3. Discuss the difference between "praying without ceasing" and following Jesus' example of frequently going off by Himself to be alone with God.
4. What did you learn in this chapter that you can adapt to your own personal time alone with God?
5. Read Psalm 42:1-2. Does this describe the degree of thirst our souls experience in our desire to be with God?

Chapter 7: Living with a Grateful Heart

1. Describe your ability to live consistently with a grateful heart.
2. Read Luke 17:11-19. After having been healed from such a physically, emotionally, and culturally devastating disease, why do you think only one leper returned to thank Jesus?
3. How does humility, and our ability to truly see (with the eyes of our hearts) God's love, mercy, and grace, affect our level of gratitude?
4. Can we easily see God at work in the daily circumstances of our lives, or is it easier to sense that, more often than not, God has left us to fend for ourselves?
5. What can we tangibly do to help nurture a grateful heart?

Chapter 8: Waiting Patiently

1. Describe when, despite intensive prayer, you endured a prolonged time of waiting for God to intervene.

2. What did you learn about God? What did you learn about yourself?

3. Recall, and then discuss, a few of the numerous examples in the Bible where God's people waited a long time for Him to fulfill a promise or to act on behalf of their suffering.

4. What did they learn? Did it impact their faith? Did it draw them closer to God or did it distance them from God?

5. How can *waiting patiently* become a lifestyle?

Chapter 9: Encouraging Each Other

1. Is it easier for you to encourage someone, or to point out their "opportunities for improvement"?

2. Describe an experience when someone's encouragement positively impacted your life.

3. Read 1 Samuel 30:1-6. In one of David's darkest hours, how was he able to strengthen or encourage himself? What did he "do"? His strength came from God, but how did he internalize it and then live in that strength?

4. How much thought and prayer do we usually give to encouraging others?

5. How much of a part does pride play in our reluctance to encourage?

Chapter 10: Standing Firm

1. Do you give much serious thought to protecting yourself from our spiritual enemy?

2. Read 2 Corinthians 11:14. If Satan masquerades as an angel of light, how do we know when it is Satan speaking to us or God speaking to us?

3. Read Ephesians 6:10-18. Discuss the parts of the armor of God. How do they, in a practical way, help us fight against our unseen but very real adversary?

4. In what way is God's Word both an offensive and defensive weapon against the devil?

5. How might it change our lives if we truly believed that our prayers for each other make an impact on our ability to stand firm?

Acknowledgments

First and foremost, I am abundantly thankful to the Holy Spirit (the true author of this book) who led me, counseled me, encouraged me, taught me, and inspired my mind and heart during this entire book-writing process.

As I completed each chapter, Donna Frueh, Tim Kuhn, Daniel Moerschel, Alice Stoddard, Cheryl Stoddard, and Margaret Stoddard all faithfully and generously gave of their time to read and comment on it. I am so thankful for their encouragement and advice. It was their kind, supportive, inspiring, and motivating words that kept me typing. Despite being ready to quit on several occasions, their consistent affirmation repeatedly drew me back to the keyboard.

I am indebted to my forty-nine-year friendship with Daniel Moerschel, our countless hours of discussion, and his gentle, persistent encouragement to write this book. When gentle persistence failed, one day over lunch, he finally, with friendly exasperation, asked me, "So when are you going to start writing your book?!" The following week I sat down at the computer and began to type.

I am also indebted to the authors of the hundreds of books I've read over the last few years. Each has planted seeds in my mind and heart that have germinated, grown, and born fruit. Their ideas, thoughts, convictions, and inspiration informed my thinking, changed my perspective, and helped my heart to see more clearly. As the author of Ecclesiastes wrote many years ago, "There is nothing new under the sun" (1:9), so, none of my thoughts are original but are an amalgamation of the thoughts of hundreds of individuals who have lived over the last few centuries.

Marilee Elash's friendship and literary expertise have been invaluable. She carefully and methodically reviewed each chapter, hunted for typos, patiently corrected my grammatical errors, and offered vital advice on how to more effectively communicate. I am very grateful for our friendship that gave her the liberty to make comments such as, "I've read this paragraph over six times, and I still don't know what you are trying to say." The quality level of this book was significantly elevated as a result of Marilee's tireless attention to detail.

I am especially thankful for my wife, Cheryl. Many of her desired home improvement projects are still on the "To Do" list because I've been typing instead of hammering. Writing this book has only been possible because of her love, affirmation, under-standing, and patience.

Notes

Introduction

1. Laura Hillenbrand, *Seabiscuit: An American Legend* (New York: The Random House Publishing Group, 2001), 52.
2. Ibid., 53.
3. Ibid.
4. Ibid., 117.
5. Ibid., 54.
6. National Museum of Racing and Hall of Fame, https://www.racingmuseum.org/hall-of-fame/seabiscuit (accessed June 18, 2018).
7. For more information related to the thoughts written in these introductory comments, visit the website: https://www.ridgelandchurch.org/hh/ where I addressed this in more detail at the time I established the Healthy Hearts Ministries in 2006 as an outreach of Ridgeland Community Church.
8. Frederick Buechner, *The Remarkable Ordinary: How to Stop, Look, and Listen to Life* (Grand Rapids: Zondervan, 2017), 36-37.

Chapter 1: Remembering God's Acts of Grace

1. David E. Garland, *Luke, vol. 3 of Exegetical Commentary on the New Testament* (Grand Rapids: Zondervan, 2011), 856.
2. Jeffrey D. Arthurs, *Preaching as Reminding: Stirring Memory in an Age of Forgetfulness* (Downers Grove, IL: InterVarsity Press, 2017), 56.

3. John D. Garr, *Living Emblems: Ancient Symbols of Faith* (Atlanta: Golden Key Press, 2007), 26.

4. Ibid., 25.

5. Ibid., 45.

6. *Mounce's Complete Expository Dictionary of Old and New Testament Words*, ed. William D. Mounce (Grand Rapids; Zondervan, 2006), 577.

7. Ian Pitt-Watson in Arthurs, x.

8. Robert Cosand in Arthurs, 13.

Chapter 2: Enriching Our Understanding of God through Metaphors

1. Spiros Zodhiates Th.D., *The Complete Word Study Dictionary New Testament* (Chattanooga: AMG Publishers, 1992), 170.

2. Brennan Manning, *Abba's Child: The Cry of the Heart for Intimate Belonging* (Colorado Springs: NavPress, 2002), 98.

3. Ralph Keyes, *The Quote Verifier: Who said What, Where, and When* (New York: St. Martin's Griffin, 2006), 164-165.

4. Merriam Webster's Collegiate Dictionary, 10th ed. (Springfield: Merriam-Webster, Incorporated, 1993), s.v. "Metaphor."

5. Eerdmans Dictionary of the Bible, ed. David Noel Freedman (Grand Rapids: Wm. B. Eerdmans Publishing Company, 2000), s.v. "Tower".

6. Warren Baker, D.R.E. and Eugene Carpenter, Ph.D., *The Complete WordStudy Dictionary Old Testament* (Chattanooga: AMG Publishers, 2003), 426.

7. James Strong, LL.D., S.T.D., The *New Strong's Exhaustive Concordance of the Bible* (Nashville: Thomas Nelson Publishers, 1990), H7682.

8. Ruth Haley Barton, *Strengthening the Soul of Your Leadership: Seeking God in the Crucible of Ministry* (Downers Grove, IL: InterVarsity Press, 2008), 145.

9. *New International Bible Dictionary*, ed. Merrill C. Tenney (Grand Rapids: Zondervan, 1987), s.v. "Cistern."

10. *Mounce's Complete Expository Dictionary of Old and New Testament Words*, ed. William D. Mounce (Grand Rapids; Zondervan, 2006), 893.

11. "Peshtigo Fire," Wikipedia, https://en.wikipedia.org/wiki/Peshtigo_fire, (accessed November 13, 2019).

12. "Great Chicago Fire," Wikipedia, https://en.wikipedia.org/wiki/Great_Chicago_Fire, (accessed November 13, 2019).

13. Eerdmans, s.v. "Birds."

14. Zodhiates, 408.

Chapter 3: Enriching Our Understanding of the Church through Metaphors

1. Philip Yancey, *Soul Survivor: How My Faith Survived the Church* (New York: Doubleday, 2001).

2. Ibid., 7.

3. "Grace Community Bible Church, Pastor Dan Burrus Blog July 19, 2018, https://gracelakeville.org/i-love-jesus-but-hate-the-church (accessed June 2, 2020).

4. Spiros Zodhiates Th.D., *The Complete Word Study Dictionary New Testament* (Chattanooga: AMG Publishers, 1992), 1252.

5. Ibid., 1254.

6. "The Return of the King" is the third and final film in "The Lord of the Rings" series produced and directed by Peter Jackson, New Line Cinema, Burbank, CA, 2003.

7. *Mounce's Complete Expository Dictionary of Old and New Testament Words*, ed. William D. Mounce (Grand Rapids; Zondervan, 2006), 110.

8. See the previous chapter for a discussion on the meaning of metaphors.

9. Eerdmans Dictionary of the Bible, ed. David Noel Freedman (Grand Rapids: Wm. B. Eerdmans Publishing Company, 2000), s.v. "Bride of Christ".

10. Saint Augustine as quoted in Paul Brand and Philip Yancey, *Fearfully and Wonderfully Made: A Surgeon Looks at the Human & Spiritual Body* (Minneapolis: Grason, 1980), 5.

11. Richard B. Hayes, *First Corinthians, Interpretation: A Bible Commentary for Teaching and Preaching* (Louisville, John Knox Press, 1997), 213.

12. Eugene H. Peterson, *Subversive Spirituality* (Grand Rapids: William B. Eerdmans Publishing Company, 1997), 124.

13. https://www.google.com/search?q=ben+-franklin+quotes+sundial+in+the+shade&rlz=1C1GCEA_enUS770US770&oq=ben+franklin+quotes+sundial+in+the+shade&aqs=chrome..69i57j33.10839j0j7&-sourceid=chrome&ie=UTF-8 (accessed June 22, 2020).

14. Henry Ford as quoted in John Maxwell, *The Five Levels of Leadership: Proven Steps to Maximize Your Potential* (New York: Hachette Book Group, 2011), 102.

15. Henri Nouwen as quoted in Brennan Manning, *Souvenirs of Solitude: Finding Rest in Abba's Embrace* (Colorado Springs: NavPress, 2009), 78.

Chapter 4: Grieving with Hope

1. Frederick Buechner, *The Sacred Journey: A Memoir of Early Days* (New York: HarperCollins Publishers, 1982), 41.

2. Nicholas Wolterstorff, Lament *for a Son* (Grand Rapids: Wm. B. Eerdmans Publishing Company, 1987), 31.

3. *Mounce's Complete Expository Dictionary of Old and New Testament Words*, ed. William D. Mounce (Grand Rapids; Zondervan, 2006), 340.

4. Spiros Zodhiates Th.D., *The Complete Word Study Dictionary New Testament* (Chattanooga: AMG Publishers, 1992), 570.

5. Mounce, 518.

6. Ibid., 426.

7. Warren Baker, D.R.E. and Eugene carpenter, Ph.D., *The Complete WordStudy Dictionary Old Testament* (Chattanooga: AMG Publishers, 2003), 360.

8. Frederick Buechner, A Crazy Holy Grace: The Healing Power of Pain and Memory (Grand Rapids: Zondervan, 2017), 65.

9. Ibid., 137.

Chapter 5: Trusting God

1. Warren Baker, D.R.E. and Eugene carpenter, Ph.D., *The Complete WordStudy Dictionary Old Testament* (Chattanooga: AMG Publishers, 2003), 18.

2. *Mounce's Complete Expository Dictionary of Old and New Testament Words*, ed. William D. Mounce (Grand Rapids; Zondervan, 2006), 746.

3. Ibid.

4. James Strong, LL.D., S.T.D., The *New Strong's Exhaustive Concordance of the Bible* (Nashville: Thomas Nelson Publishers, 1990), H982.

5. Baker, 782.

6. Mounce, 1002.

7. Strong, H2620.

Chapter 6: Spending Time Alone with God

1. Thomas Keating in Brennan Manning, *Ruthless Trust: The Ragamuffin's Path to God* (New York: HarperCollins Publishers, 2000), 130.
2. A.W. Tozer in John Eldredge, *The Journey of Desire: Searching for the Life We've Only Dreamed Of* (Nashville: Thomas Nelson Publishers, 2000), 57.
3. *Mounce's Complete Expository Dictionary of Old and New Testament Words*, ed. William D. Mounce (Grand Rapids; Zondervan, 2006), 532.
4. Spiros Zodhiates Th.D., *The Complete Word Study Dictionary New Testament* (Chattanooga: AMG Publishers, 1992), 399.
5. Ibid., 1230.
6. Mother Teresa, https://www.goodreads.com/quotes/128334-prayer-is-not-asking-prayer-is-putting-oneself-in-the, (accessed November 20, 2019).
7. Eugene H. Peterson, *Eat This Book: A Conversation in the Art of Spiritual Reading* (Grand Rapids: William B. Eerdmans Publishing Company, 2006), 108.
8. M. Robert Mulholland Jr., *Shaped by the Word: The Power of Scripture in Spiritual Formation* Revised edition (Nashville: Upper Room Books, 2000), 147.
9. Eugene H. Peterson, *Subversive Spirituality* (Grand Rapids: William B. Eerdmans Publishing Company, 1997), 37.
10. Karl Rayner in Brennan Manning, *The Relentless Tenderness of Jesus* (Grand Rapids: Fleming H. Revell, 2004), 12.
11. Amy and Judge Reinhold, comp., *Be Still and Know that I Am God: 31 Days to a Deeper Meditative Prayer Life* (New York: Howard Books, 2007), 12-20.

12. Ruth Haley Barton, *Sacred Rhythms: Arranging Our Lives for Spiritual Transformation* (Downers Grove, IL: InterVarsity Press, 2006), 54-61.

13. Dallas Willard, *Hearing God: Developing a Conversational Relationship with God* (Downers Grove: InterVarsity Press, 1999), 88.

14. "Buddhism," Wikipedia, https://en.m.wikipedia.org/wiki/Buddhism (accessed December 2, 2019).

15. "Transcendentalism," Wikipedia, https://en.m.wikipedia.org/wiki/Transcendentalism (accessed December 2, 2019).

16. "New Age," Wikipedia, https://en.m.wikipedia.org/wiki/New_Age (accessed December 2, 2019).

17. Mounce, 922.

18. I am not sure where I read or heard Rick quote this. I believe it was in a seminar in which he spoke.

19. In 2006, I read this in an article written by Henri Nouwen, but, despite a thorough search, am unable to locate the source.

20. http://www.geneseeabbey.org/

21. Brennan Manning, *The Relentless Tenderness of Jesus* (Grand Rapids: Fleming H. Revell, 2004), 9-10.

Chapter 7: Living with a Grateful Heart

1. Spiros Zodhiates Th.D., *The Complete Word Study Dictionary New Testament* (Chattanooga: AMG Publishers, 1992), 99, 1461.

2. James Strong, LL.D., S.T.D., The *New Strong's Exhaustive Concordance of the Bible* (Nashville: Thomas Nelson Publishers, 1990), G3173.

3. Read 2 Kings 17:6, 24.

4. Claus Westermann in Frederick J. Gaiser, "Your Faith has Made You Well: Healing and Salvation in Luke 17:12-19," Word and World, vol. XVI, number 3, summer 1996, 295. https://pdfs.

semanticscholar.org/b44b/f2242261d106dbe3ba99ef9b-074cf944bc68.pdf (PDF file accessed September 30, 2018)

5. R. Alan Culpepper, *The Gospel of Luke, vol. 9 of The New Interpreter's Bible: A Commentary in Twelve Volumes* (Nashville: Abingdon Press, 1995), 328.

6. Bob Stoddard, *Daily Journal: April 12, 2009-July 31, 2009*, vol. 11, 6/26/09.

7. Ibid.

8. Elizabeth Dreyer, *Earth Crammed with Heaven: A Spirituality of Everyday Life* (Mahwah, NJ: Paulist Press, 1994), 23.

9. Ruth Haley Barton, *Strengthening the Soul of Your Leadership: Seeking God in the Crucible of Ministry* (Downers Grove, IL: InterVarsity Press, 2008), 63.

10. Ibid., 62.

11. Elizabeth Barrett Browning in Barton, 64.

Chapter 8: Waiting Patiently

1. John Ortberg, *The Life You've Always Wanted: Spiritual Disciplines for Ordinary People* (Grand Rapids: Zondervan, 1997, 2002), 76.

2. Warren Baker, D.R.E. and Eugene carpenter, Ph.D., *The Complete WordStudy Dictionary Old Testament* (Chattanooga: AMG Publishers, 2003), 343.

3. Mounce's, 935.

4. Willem A. VanGemeren, *Psalms*, vol. 5 of *The Expositor's Bible Commentary* (Grand Rapids: Zondervan Publishing House, 1991), 483.

5. Zodhiates, 536.

6. Bob Stoddard, *Daily Journal: July 1-December 31, 2016*, vol. 26, 7/2/16.

7. Ibid., 8/23/16.

8. Ibid., 8/24/16.
9. Ibid., 8/26/16.
10. Ibid., 10/5/16.
11. Ibid., 10/31/16.
12. Ibid., 11/10/16.
13. Ibid., 11/26/16.
14. Henri J. M. Nouwen, *The Path of Waiting* (New York: The Crossroad Publishing Company, 1995), 6.
15. Pete Wilson, *"Spiritual Transformation Happens in the Waiting Room,"* http://www.petewilson.tv/2016/02/25/spiritual-transformation-happens-in-the-waiting-room/ (accessed August 21, 2018).
16. Matthew Lee Anderson, *The End of Our Exploring* (Chicago: Moody Publishers, 2013), 119.

Chapter 9: Encouraging Each Other

1. Jess Lair in Dale Carnegie, *Pathways to Success* (Hauppauge, NY: Dale Carnegie and Associates, Inc., 1964), 213.
2. Dallas Willard, *The Divine Conspiracy: Rediscovering our Hidden Life in God* (New York: HarperCollins, 1998), 218.
3. Everett Shostrom in his book *Man, The Manipulator* as quoted in John Maxwell,
4. *The Five Levels of Leadership* (New York: Hachette Book Group, 2011), 192.
5. Edward W. Goodrick and John R. Kohlenberger III, *The Strongest NIV Exhaustive Concordance* (Grand Rapids: Zondervan, 1999), 4138.
6. See: Deut. 1:38, Deut. 3:28, Judg. 20:22, 2 Sam. 11:25, Ps. 64:5, Isa. 41:7.
7. See chapter, "Spending Time Alone with God" for further discussion on meditation.

8. Online dictionary https://www.google.com/search?q=-consolation&rlz=1C1GCEA_enUS770US770&oq=-cons&aqs=chrome.1.69i57j69i59j0l6.3710j1j7&sourceid=-chrome&ie=UTF-8 (accessed January 20, 2020)

9. Jerry Sittser, *A Grace Disguised: How the Soul Grows Through Loss* (Grand Rapids: Zondervan, 2004).

10. Brennan Manning, *All is Grace: A Ragamuffin Memoir* (Colorado Springs: David C. Cook, 2011).

11. Peter Scazzero, *Emotionally Healthy Spirituality: Unleash a Revolution in Your Life in Christ* (Nashville: Integrity Publishers, 2006).

12. See: Deut. 1:38, Deut 3:28, Judg. 20:22, 2 Sam. 11:25 Ps. 64:5, Isa. 41:7.

13. *Mounce's Complete Expository Dictionary of Old and New Testament Words*, ed. William D. Mounce (Grand Rapids; Zondervan, 2006), 134.

14. Fred B. Craddck, *The Letter to the Hebrews, vol. 12 of The New Interpreter's Bible: A Commentary in Twelve Volumes* (Nashville: Abingdon Press, 1995), 121.

15. Leon Morris, *Hebrews*, vol. 12 of *The Expositor's Bible Commentary* (Grand Rapids: Zondervan Publishing House, 1991), 105.

16. Spiros Zodhiates Th.D., *The Complete Word Study Dictionary New Testament* (Chattanooga: AMG Publishers, 1992), 1122.

Chapter 10: Standing Firm

1. "Civil War Facts," American Battlefield Trust, https://www.battlefields.org/learn/articles/civil-war-facts#How%20many%20soldiers%20died%20in%20the%20Civil%20War? (Accessed April 17, 2020).]

2. Ibid.

3. Ibid.
4. *Florence Nightingale: A Life Inspired* Kindle Edition (Wyatt North Publishing, LLC, 2015).
5. Ibid.
6. "Girolamo Fracastoro," *Encyclopedia Britannica*, https://www. britannica.com/biography/Girolamo-Fracastoro (Accessed April 17, 2020).
7. "Germ Theory of Disease," *Wikipedia*, https://en.wikipedia. org/wiki/Germ_theory_of_disease (Accessed April 17, 2020).
8. "Louis Pasteur," *Encyclopedia Britannica*, https://www.britan-nica.com/biography/Louis-Pasteur (Accessed April 17, 2020).
9. As frequently reported on CBS News, March-May 2020.
10. C. S. Lewis, *The Screwtape Letters* (Uhrichsville, Ohio: Barbour Publishing, Inc., 1985).
11. Ibid, p. 16-17.
12. Ibid, p. 20.
13. Ibid, p. 17.
14. Ibid, p. 31.
15. Spiros Zodhiates Th.D., *The Complete Word Study Dictionary New Testament* (Chattanooga: AMG Publishers, 1992), 972-973.
16. A question may arise whether we are to flee the devil or resist the devil. The apostle Paul instructed Timothy to "Flee the evil desires of youth, and pursue righteousness, faith, love and peace, along with those who call on the Lord out of a pure heart" (1 Tim. 2:22, NIV). Read the story of Joseph (Gen. 37-50). Out of jealousy, envy, and ultimately anger, his brothers sold him to a band of Ishmaelites who took him to Egypt where Potipher, the captain of Pharaoh's guard bought him as a slave, placed him in charge of his entire household, and "entrusted to his care everything he owned" (Gen. 39:4, NIV). It was not long before Potipher's wife took notice of Joseph and attempted to seduce him. At first he resisted and refused her, but one day

she approached him while all the household servants were outside. Grabbing his cloak she urged him to join her in the bedroom. This time he left his cloak in her hands and fled the house. Joseph was a man of integrity and refused to be seduced by his master's wife. He knew how to resist the devil by fleeing from a compromising situation.

17. Ted Slampyak, "How to Gird Up Your Loins: An Illustrated Guide," Get Action AOM, https://www.artofmanliness.com/articles/how-to-gird-up-your-loins-an-illustrated-guide/ (accessed April 21, 2020).

18. Zodhiates, 458.

19. Dallas Willard, *Life Without Lack: Living in the Fullness of Psalm 23* (Nashville: Thomas Nelson, 2018), 169.

20. Dallas Willard, *The Divine Conspiracy: Rediscovering our Hidden Life in God* (New York: HarperCollins, 1998), 219.

21. Brennan Manning, *Ruthless Trust: The Ragamuffin's Path to God* (New York: HarperCollins Publishers, 2002).

22. *Mounce's Complete Expository Dictionary of Old and New Testament Words*, ed. William D. Mounce (Grand Rapids; Zondervan, 2006), 232.

23. Ibid., 701.

24. Eugene H. Peterson, *Working the Angles: The Shape of Pastoral Integrity* (Grand Rapids: William B. Eerdmans Publishing Company, 1987), 192.

25. [Frank C. Laubach, *Prayer: The Mightiest Force in the World* (Old Tappan, New Jersey: Fleming H. Revell Company, 1946), 34.

About the Author

B ob, the son of missionaries, grew up in Guatemala. He graduated from Houghton College in 1972 with a BS in Biology, and then graduated from Physician Assistant training at Albany Medical College in 1977. After serving for over thirty years as a Pediatric PA, he returned to school and graduated from Northeastern Seminary with a MA in Theology. He served as the pastor of a small non-denominational church for six years before retiring in November 2015. He and his wife, Cheryl, recently moved to Orchard Park, NY, to be closer to their two grandchildren.

Visit: www.bobstoddard.com

CPSIA information can be obtained
at www.ICGtesting.com
Printed in the USA
LVHW050223040621
689239LV00014B/1532